COMMONSENSE
CATALOGING

ROSALIND E. MILLER AND JANE C. TERWILLEGAR

COMMONSENSE CATALOGING

A CATALOGER'S MANUAL

THIRD EDITION

THE H. W. WILSON COMPANY · 1983 · NEW YORK

Printed in the United States of America

Library of Congress Cataloging in Publication Data

Miller, Rosalind E.
    Commonsense cataloging.

    Rev. ed. of: Commonsense cataloging / Esther J.
Piercy. 2nd. ed. 1974.
    Bibliography: p.
    Includes index.
    1. Cataloging.   I. Terwillegar, Jane C.   II. Piercy,
Esther J.   Commonsense cataloging.   III. Title.
Z693.M54   1983   025.3   83-1306
ISBN 0-8242-0689-4

TABLE OF CONTENTS

PREFACE TO THE THIRD EDITION

THE FIRST EDITION of *Commonsense Cataloging*, published in 1965, was intended to serve as a manual for the beginning cataloger, trained or untrained. In her preface Esther H. Piercy expressed the hope that the book would "dispel some of the fears, mystery, superstitions, and mystique which sometimes surround the word cataloging," enabling the librarian to "decide, first, what purposes the collection is intended to serve, and then how best to organize the materials to perform the services." Although the past 18 years have seen the proliferation of non-print materials in libraries, the growth of cataloging services, and an increase in the use of computers, the task of the cataloger has not essentially changed, and the purpose of the first edition remains valid. The third edition of *Commonsense Cataloging* is an entirely new book, but its authors have built on the foundation laid by the first edition, combining an account of new developments in cataloging with a commonsense approach.

The method of the first edition, which proceeded from the "general to the specific, and from principles to practices" has also been retained, except in cases where innovations have dictated otherwise. In the revised cataloging code, problems of description are addressed before principles of entry. This change has been reflected in the book. Because prepared copy is now available to almost all librarians, little space is devoted to typing rules and more to the adaptation of prepared copy to meet the needs of a particular collection. Non-print materials are now a major resource of many libraries, so cataloging rules for these formats are no longer given in a separate chapter, but discussed in the same context as printed documents.

Technical cataloging terms, which are printed in small capitals, are defined in the glossary.

We gratefully acknowledge the assistance of colleagues and friends: Richard Reeb of the Pullen Library at Georgia State University, who gave expert technical advice; Stephen Cox, who took the photographs; Linda Montgomery and Olivia Carlisle, who typed the manuscript; and Pheon Sinclair, who undertook innumerable tasks associated with the project. We also thank our many students, whose enthusiasm encouraged us to write this book.

The Forest Press, the Baker & Taylor Company, the Minnesota Educational Computing Consortium, and the Online Computer Library Center have kindly allowed us permission to reproduce excerpts from their publications.

ROSALIND E. MILLER
JANE C. TERWILLEGAR

Atlanta, Georgia
West Palm Beach, Florida
March 1983

AT HIS DEATH in 1519, Leonardo da Vinci left more than 10,000 sheets of manuscript recording a lifetime's speculation and research in art, mathematics, biology, engineering, and architecture. Of this extraordinary record of genius only some 7,000 sheets are known to have survived, but it is hoped that the remainder were not destroyed and will someday reappear. Hence the excitement when, in 1967, Professor Jules Piccus of the University of Massachusetts discovered two leather-bound volumes containing 700 sheets of Leonardo's notebooks in the National Library of Madrid. The presence of these volumes in the library had long been known: they were recorded in the catalog but had been mis-shelved during the 19th century and several searches had failed to bring them to light. Professor Piccus, looking for medieval ballads, had stumbled on them accidentally. The head of the Madrid library, embarrassed by the international attention that was drawn to the negligence of a long-dead shelver, lamely defended his institution by explaining that they would, in any case, have been discovered eventually.

Few errors of librarianship have such momentous consequences, and catalogers rarely have the responsibility of classifying and shelving materials of such value, but the incident in Madrid is a striking demonstration of the fact that an item misplaced is an item lost to the patrons of the library. The student unable to find a certain work of literary criticism, the teacher searching in vain for a filmstrip, and the who-done-it enthusiast asking for "another by the same author," find inadequate cataloging as frustrating as it was to the librarians in Madrid looking for the lost Leonardos.

There are information needs at each stage of life, from the pre-schooler developing listening skills during story hour to the elderly citizen seeking both recreational and informational materials. If, at any stage in the search, a seeker of information becomes frustrated, the library has failed in its purpose. Collections must be effectively organized so that patrons can find what has been selected for their use.

At first sight, modern cataloging practice may seem dauntingly complex. Information is now packaged in forms unknown a brief time ago; the rules of descriptive cataloging have been altered; and computer technology is changing cataloging processes even in small libraries. But these innovations have changed only the form, not the basic function of catalogs, which exist to guide users of library resources to the materials that answer their needs.

As librarians look forward to the information needs and technologies of the 21st century, the opportunities and challenges of their profession increase, as does the need for competent catalogers. Computers now make it possible to link all libraries, large and small, through their catalogs. Incorrect and illogical cataloging practice can impede the building of a vast information network. Today's catalogers may find themselves in almost any type of work environment, from being the only professional staff member, responsible for all library activities, to serving as part of a large cataloging team. Whatever the situation, a librarian with an understanding of basic terminology, cataloging principles, and practical application, will find more professional challenges than ever before.

CHAPTER 1

PAST TO PRESENT: LIBRARY CATALOGS

CIVILIZATION began when the invention of writing made it possible for societies to record their knowledge. Once people learned that by drawing pictures or making stylus marks on clay they could keep track of such matters as taxes due or the correct form of religious rituals, the need for storing and organizing this information for future reference became obvious. Thus, as soon as libraries were established catalogers became a necessity, and early librarians, called by the Assyrians "men of the written tablets," had responsibilities very similar to those of catalogers today.

ORGANIZING LIBRARY COLLECTIONS: A CATALOGER'S ART

From the earliest days, inventory records were kept of materials housed in an individual collection. For many centuries the primary role of librarians was to guard this stored material, and they were held officially responsible if any item was misplaced. Today many libraries still take annual inventories and report how many items have slipped away.

The file, or catalog, used to take this inventory is a list arranged in the same order as materials are stored on the shelf; and called the SHELF LIST. Since ancient times this type of record has been considered essential. A small library might do without other records, but there should always be a shelf list to answer the question asked by an inventory, "What materials are in this collection?"

Libraries of Babylonia and Assyria were far from small, however. They held thousands of clay tablets concerning subjects as diverse as taxation, law, literature, and religion. A simple shelf-list catalog was not adequate because it could not provide the answer to questions about the location of tablets on monument building or other specific topics. As a result, arrangement by subject was developed, and catalogs were kept for each subject. CALL NUMBERS were used to find these tablets; that is, each tablet was marked with a location symbol that was also recorded in the catalog listing. Works were further identified by title, and often annotations (brief descriptions of the contents) were added to the record. So, thousands of years ago, at Nineveh and Akkad, cataloging became an established art. These records were similar to those that we now find in modern library catalogs.

A library catalog provides:

a shelf list, providing an inventory of the collection
call numbers, for locating the position of items on the shelves
classification, for shelving like items together within a subject field
subject headings, for determining specific topics
descriptive cataloging, for identifying and describing individual items

During the 5th century AD, when the Roman Empire was destroyed by barbarian invaders, most libraries, including the great collection made by Constantine at Byzantium, were pillaged or left to decay. Fragments of classical libraries survived in churches and monasteries, however, and from these texts evolved the learning of the European Renaissance. Some medieval and Renaissance monastic and private libraries grew to considerable size and manuscript catalogs in the form of books were produced to make their contents accessible to users. With few exceptions, however, these catalogs remained simple inventories with call numbers; not until the 17th century did cataloging under title and author's name become relatively common. The catalog of the Bodleian Library in Oxford, made in 1674, was probably the first to contain a shelf list, an alphabetical index of authors' names, and rudimentary classification by subject. Cataloging in the modern sense — providing access to materials by their authorship, title, subject, and form — was a creation of 19th-century librarians working in Britain, the United States, and Europe.

Since the third millenium BC ways of preserving a permanent record of knowledge have evolved far beyond the papyrus roll and the clay tablet. One can now retrieve information from books, films, microforms, tapes, or computer discs, but librarians must still organize the materials in their collections so that similar information in a subject field is shelved together (CLASSIFICATION); give each item a prescribed shelf location (CALL NUMBERS); arrange items according to their subjects (SUBJECT HEADINGS); provide clear descriptions of materials so that they can be distinguished (DESCRIPTIVE CATALOGING); and keep an inventory of the collection (SHELF LIST).

According to the size and scope of the collection, some catalogs are more detailed and extensive than others. Before the invention of printing, books were copied by hand and the cost and laboriousness of this process limited the size of libraries. An inventory, or shelf list, was adequate for all but a few collections. This might still be true today in a small rental library, where patrons mainly browse for leisure reading. In special libraries, where users' requests are frequently answered with specific subject bibliographies, the emphasis is on subject analysis. In a rare book collection the careful description of valuable items is of prime importance. No matter what types of materials are collected, the cataloger must organize them so that knowledge can be retrieved.

A CATALOGER'S TOOL KIT

If everyone were assigned to a particular library at birth, and could use only that library for their entire lifetime, there would be little need for cataloging tools. All libraries could be arranged differently without inconvenience to their users. In reality, however, people use many different libraries, and media and information centers during their lives. Libraries share resources through inter-library loan, and now have ways of linking collections together by computer networks. Consequently, there have been many efforts to standardize classification and cataloging procedures. Standard procedures allow librarians to catalog and organize collections, and readers to use them, in more than one library.

A standard classification schedule is essential for grouping materials within subject areas.

CLASSIFICATION

Dewey, Melvil. *Abridged Dewey Decimal Classification and Relative Index.*
Ed. 11. Edited under the direction of Benjamin A. Custer. Albany, N.Y.: Forest Press, Division of Lake Placid Education Foundation, 1979.

Dewey, Melvil. *Dewey Decimal Classification and Relative Index.* Ed. 19. Edited under the direction of Benjamin A. Custer. Albany, N.Y.: Forest Press, Division of Lake Placid Education Foundation, 1979.

Library of Congress Classification Schedules: A Cumulation of Additions and Changes. Detroit: Gale Research Company, 1974-.

Library of Congress. Subject Cataloging Division. *Classification.* 34 vols. Washington, D.C.: Library of Congress, 1901-.

3

Most school and public libraries are arranged according to the Dewey Classification Schedules (DDC), and academic libraries according to the Library of Congress system (LCC). Small general libraries commonly use the abridged version of Dewey.

SUBJECT
HEADINGS

A standard subject heading list is used to select uniform headings so that the catalog can be used to locate particular topics.

> *Sears List of Subject Headings.* 12th ed. Barbara M. Westby, ed. New York: The H. W. Wilson Company, 1982.

> Library of Congress, Subject Cataloging Division. *Library of Congress Subject Headings.* 9th ed. Washington, D.C.: Library of Congress, 1980. (With quarterly supplements accumulated annually. Also available in microform with the entire list cumulated quarterly.)

Large collections and those using LC classification will use the LC Subject Heading List (LCSH). Small public and school libraries usually take their headings from *Sears.* Special collections devoted exclusively to acquisition of materials on a single topic, such as medicine or religion, often use uniform lists developed for that particular subject field.

DESCRIPTIVE
CATALOGING
CODES

Items are described according to the precise specifications of a cataloging code so that they may be distinguished from one another. These rules provide guidance for recording BIBLIOGRAPHIC DETAILS such as names, titles, editions, publishers; and for PHYSICAL DESCRIPTIONS, such as number of pages, or size of film.

> *Anglo-American Cataloging Rules.* 2nd ed. Prepared by the American Library Association, the British Library, the Canadian Committee of Cataloguing, the Library Association, the Library of Congress. Michael Gorman and Paul W. Winkler, eds. Chicago: American Library Association, 1978.

> Gorman, Michael. *The Concise AACR2.* Chicago, American Library Association, 1981.

Using these basic tools, librarians can describe materials so that users can identify and select items from the catalog description (AACR2); can place items in shelf locations adjacent to other materials dealing with the same topic (DDC or LCC); and provide more precise subject access by using the standard subject heading list (*Sears* or LCSH).

In addition to these general tools, some libraries make use of other aids developed for special collections. For example, libraries that house only slides may follow more detailed rules for their descriptions; special collections in particular subject fields may use alternative subject heading lists; and a number of libraries have developed their own classification schemes or use other recognized systems like the Universal Dewey Classification. For the most part, however, the tools listed in this chapter are those commonly used in general collections.

THE CATALOG'S FORM

Although the basic information has not changed, the form of the library's catalog has varied widely since ancient days. Assyrian inventories were made on clay tablets, Egyptian records were carved on the library walls, medieval collections were listed in BOOK CATALOGS, and during the 19th century CARD CATALOGS became popular. The idea of a UNION CATALOG, a listing of the holdings of more than one collection, was first proposed during the 13th century. Today we also have MICROFORM CATALOGS and ON-LINE COMPUTER CATALOGS. Since computers can communicate with each other, it is now possible by NET-WORKING to have centralized on-line catalogs of collections scattered throughout the nation. As computer costs drop, it is possible that the on-line catalog will eventually become as ubiquitous as the card catalog is now.

Although the card catalog is not the oldest form, it has certainly been the most popular. Its advantages were first recognized at the end of the 18th century in France, when the revolutionary government confiscated large numbers of books from private collections and church libraries. Descriptions of these books made according to the French national code of 1791 were entered on slips of paper and playing cards in regional centers and mailed to the National Library in Paris, where they were arranged alphabetically by author and fastened together by a cord passed through the lower left-hand corner. This system, which allowed catalogers to interpolate or remove accessions without disturbing the catalog as a whole, did not become widely accepted until the late 19th century. When, in 1902, the Library of Congress began selling sets of printed catalog cards for a nominal fee, book catalogs rapidly

THE CARD
CATALOG

disappeared in the United States, and, although other forms were still used for special purposes, the card catalog prevailed.

The decision of the Library of Congress to sell cards had more important consequences than the disappearance of book catalogs. Until then, cataloging had been done by librarians who worked more or less independently, and made little effort to standardize procedures. Now there was a central agency providing not only printed cards, but also standards for the cataloging of every library. The cataloging practices of the Library of Congress therefore became the cataloging standards for most libraries. The Library of Congress continues to exert a strong influence to this day.

In those early years the disadvantages of card catalogs had not yet been realized. Although card catalogs grow slowly, they may reach enormous proportions in large collections, and even small libraries may find space is at a premium as they try to position the card catalog for the convenience of both the public and the library staff. Catalogs often double in size every 20 years or less; have to be housed in specially designed, expensive furniture; and require expensive maintenance, as cards are added, removed, shifted, and altered. Visit any large collection which still has a card catalog and observe the number of staff members doing little else but keeping it up to date. Furthermore, during the social unrest of the late 1960s and '70s, card catalogs proved especially vulnerable to attack by those who expressed their radical opinions by removing and destroying drawers of catalog cards.

COMPUTER-
PRODUCED
CATALOGS

Library catalogs tend to change physical form whenever technology allows another format to be made less expensively. Computers have been used to produce catalogs in a variety of forms: card, book, microform, and on-line. Before a computer can generate any sort of catalog, the record for each item must be entered in its memory, forming a data base of the library's holdings. Because this data base is indecipherable by the human eye, and cannot be browsed, computer data bases are either converted to a readable form, such as a microform or a book catalog, or accessed visually through a direct on-line computer terminal.

COMPUTER-
PRODUCED
BOOK CATALOGS

Listing the contents of a library in a ledger or notebook was one of the earliest methods of keeping an inventory. When technology allowed this information to be printed, rather than handwritten, book catalogs became standard. Produced in multiple copies, they were used for inventory, and for INTER-LIBRARY LOAN. As long as library collections grew slowly, book catalogs remained serviceable, but, as the French National Library discovered, they become inadequate once a collection has begun to grow rapidly. It is costly and difficult to produce new editions or update with supplements.

Book catalogs came into general use once again when, during the late 1960s, it became possible to print them easily and inexpensively by computer. By then card catalogs were causing space problems in many libraries and computer-produced book catalogs gained in popularity. It is possible to print a complete computer catalog for every branch library, even for each bookmobile, and copies can be shelved in classrooms, offices, and homes. Mutilation or loss of a volume is less problematic, because new ones can be printed and maintenance costs are relatively low. Cataloging records can be shortened and made simpler for the general public to use—an impractical idea when the card catalog served as the main bibliographic tool for user and librarian alike. Book catalogs can be photocopied to provide students with a complete list of titles in a subject area; and circulation has been found to increase when whole pages of material can be scanned at once, rather than one item at a time. Many predicted that the book catalog would enjoy a complete renaissance during the 1980s, but technology moves quickly, and whereas many libraries, particularly public libraries, still rely on their book catalogs, another computer-produced form has entered the field.

A microform is a photographic reproduction in miniature of printed works, blueprints, diagrams, or cataloging information that must be enlarged for reading with the aid of magnifying equipment. Two common forms are MICROFICHE, a sheet of transparent film, usually 4 x 6 inches, containing a number of images arranged in rows; and MICROFILM, a roll of transparent film, containing images arranged in a sequence. Either of these forms may be directly produced from a computer data base, creating a computer output microform catalog, or COM CAT. It is this form of catalog, rather than the book catalog, that has recently been replacing card catalogs.

COM catalogs offer many of the advantages of book catalogs: compactness, multiple copies, many entries can be viewed at once, and low maintenance requirements; and they are also much cheaper to produce. Initial investment in microform reading equipment is high, but the cost of updating and re-

COMPUTER OUTPUT MICROFORM CATALOG: COM CAT

issuing the entire catalog is low because there is no need to produce printed copy. COM Cats have grown more popular, and a number of VENDORS now offer plans for conversion and the equipment needed.

However, just as the card catalog becomes increasingly costly over the years, so does the COM Cat. Each time a vendor produces a new catalog, a charge is made, not only for each new record inserted, but for resorting all the records in the entire catalog. In time the COM catalog will be too expensive to maintain. So although COM Cats are rapidly replacing other formats, eventually they too will be replaced by superior technology.

THE ON-LINE CATALOG

A computer can both print information on paper and also display it on the screen of a video terminal. As the term "on-line" implies, the user of this system is in direct communication with the computer data base and may question it as necessary. Using a video, or cathode-ray, terminal, the data base information is retrieved by the operator using a keyboard. Cataloging records are displayed on the screen as they are called up from the data base. With careful programming users can operate terminals by themselves, rather than having to depend on the library staff.

Such a catalog is never out of date, because items are added to the data base as soon as they are acquired by the library. As yet, few libraries have on-line systems available for public use, but as technology advances and more systems offer programming designed for library patrons, this type of catalog will become more common. The decreasing cost of computer hardware and the increasing memory capacity of small personal computers make on-line catalogs an attractive possibility for even the smallest collection.

SUMMARY

Catalogers are now beginning to make use of the computer to provide access to stored information, and it is likely that this technology will supersede the card catalog, just as the card catalog replaced earlier forms. No matter what its form, the library's catalog will continue to answer basic questions about the collection, providing users with information about what is available and where it can be found. A cataloger's art then, is to organize a collection of knowledge into an intelligible system, so that specific information can be retrieved on demand.

CHAPTER REVIEW

Terms to understand:

bibliographic details	microform catalog
book catalogs	net-working
call numbers	on-line computer catalog
card catalog	Sears
classification	shelf list
COM Cat	subject headings
descriptive cataloging	union catalog
LSCH	

Functions of the catalog:

1. Shelf list provides for inventory.
2. Call numbers locate items on the shelf.
3. Classification through notation.
4. Subject heading locates subjects by specific topics.
5. Descriptive cataloging identifies and describes individual items.

Cataloger's tools:

Dewey Decimal Classification and Relative Index and *Abridged Dewey Decimal Classification and Relative Index.*
Library of Congress Classification Schedules.
Sears List of Subject Headings.
Library of Congress Subject Headings.

Forms of the catalog:

card
book
microform
on-line

CHAPTER 2

THE CATALOG RECORD

BY ANSWERING questions about the authorship, subject, and location of library materials, the catalog serves as an index to the collection. The cataloger uses tools to prepare this index so these questions are answered as accurately and efficiently as possible.

Library users often come to the catalog with partial information about what they are seeking. They may know an author's first or last name (sometimes misspelled), or some significant words in the title, or they may have a vague notion of the subject area, but be unable to translate this into the terms used by catalogers. They may even find a relevant entry, but become so confused at interpreting it they never find the item on the shelf. Catalogers try to anticipate users' problems, but this is not always easy to do.

LOCATING THE RECORD

The majority of those searching a library catalog are looking for an individual item. In order to give as much help as possible the cataloger prepares records about each item under various HEADINGS that are filed, more or less alphabetically, in the catalog. These records are called ENTRIES, and the headings under which they are found are called ACCESS POINTS, because they provide the user with access into the catalog of the collection.

Headings do more, however, than locate individual items. They are standardized so that works having common characteristics are gathered together. These gatherings make it possible to identify all of an author's works in the collection, as well as a single title; or all materials on field hockey, not just a particular book. Headings provide access to a single title such as *The Rise of Theodore Roosevelt*, and also gather all the biographies of President Theodore Roosevelt together as a group.

The question of which are the most effective headings, or access points, has long been the subject of debate among catalogers. Headings for titles and for authors' names have been agreed upon, but in certain cases the name of a corporate body

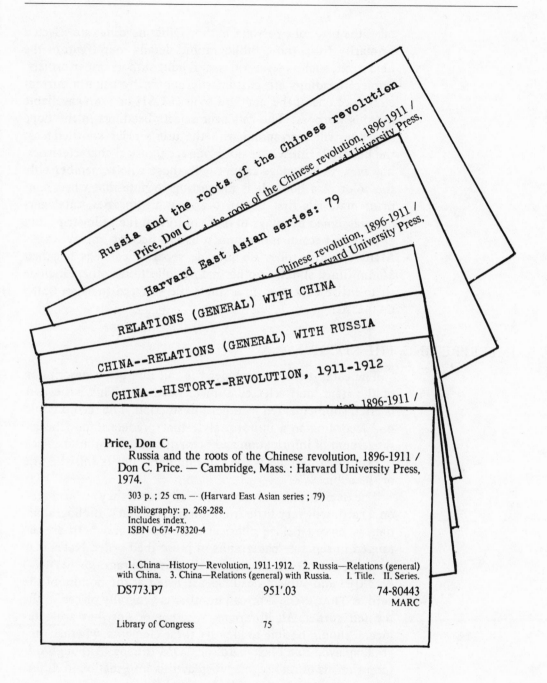

Russia and the roots of the Chinese revolution
Price, Don C

Harvard East Asian series: 79

RELATIONS (GENERAL) WITH CHINA

CHINA--RELATIONS (GENERAL) WITH RUSSIA

CHINA--HISTORY--REVOLUTION, 1911-1912

Russia and the roots of the Chinese revolution, 1896-1911 /
Don C. Price. — Cambridge, Mass. : Harvard University Press,
1974.

303 p. ; 25 cm. — (Harvard East Asian series ; 79)

Bibliography: p. 268-288.
Includes index.
ISBN 0-674-78320-4

1. China—History—Revolution, 1911-1912.   2. Russia—Relations (general)
with China.   3. China—Relations (general) with Russia.   I. Title.   II. Series.

DS773.P7   951'.03   74-80443
                                                                     MARC

Library of Congress   75

Figure 2-1

A catalog record or entry is filed under different headings, or access points   11 takes the place of a personal author. Other headings are selected primarily from those bibliographic details found within the item itself, such as series titles, and joint authors or performers. Subject headings are customarily chosen by using a current edition of one of the standard tools (LCSH or Sears) available for this purpose. The cataloger selects headings in the hope that one will correspond with the user's prior knowledge of the material. Entries are not made for physical characteristics, however, and catalogs cannot help those who remember only the color of a book. It is interesting to note that when non-print materials first began to appear in libraries, catalogers often assigned headings to types of format (i.e., filmstrip), but as formats became more numerous this became impracticable. Many libraries today do provide separate catalogs for their 16mm films, slides, or other media collections; others include their entire collection in a single file referred to as an OMNI CATALOG.

INTERPRETING THE RECORD

The catalog record provides the call number, a description of the item, and selected subject headings. This basic data is often supplemented by other information. The record is laid out according to a uniform style that predetermines the arrangement of information and prevents, or at least limits, such questions as "Which is the call number?" or "Is this the title or the subject?"

The details of this record, especially when they are arranged on a card, will vary little from library to library. Bibliographic data is placed before physical description, and both are arranged in separate paragraphs in prescribed order. Notes may be added to form an optional, third paragraph. ADDED ENTRIES and subject headings are listed at the bottom of the card as TRACINGS. The call number is generally placed in the top left corner. All librarians, whether or not they are catalogers, should be able to identify these elements, whether they are displayed in a book, card, or COM catalog. Although different forms of catalog may display this information in different ways, the basic elements do not vary.

Tracing 1 indicates there is a subject heading card filed under LANGUAGES, MODERN – STUDY AND TEACHING. In the catalog, subject headings are capitalized in order to distinguish them from added entries. There are also two added entries, indicated by roman numerals, one under the name of Gilbert A. Jarvis, who wrote the foreword to this book. His name is on the title page and the cataloger felt that someone

ELEMENTS OF A CATALOG CARD

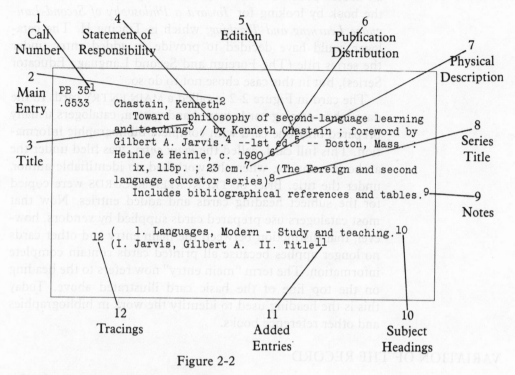

Figure 2-2

1. Call number, using LC classification.
2. Main entry, under author's last name.
3. Full title.
4. Statement of responsibility; repeat of author's name, and additional people associated with the work.
5. Edition statement.
6. Publication and distribution information, including place of publication, publisher, and date of copyright. (Formerly called the imprint.)
7. Physical description; in this case number of pages and height of book in centimeters. (Formerly called the collation.)
8. Series title; this book is one of a series on teaching foreign languages issued by this publisher.
9. Notes, consisting of information considered useful by the cataloger.
10. Subject heading, always listed by arabic numbers in the tracings.
11. Added entries or access points taken from the bibliographic details, listed by roman numerals. Names are listed before other information.
12. Cards for this book are scattered throughout the catalog under different headings. It is necessary to know how many and what cards exist for each work, so that they can be corrected or removed. This information is known as a tracing because it allows the cards to be traced.

looking for the book might remember his name and use it as an access point. Someone remembering the title could find the book by looking for *Toward a Philosophy of Second-Language Learning and Teaching,* which is Tracing II. The cataloger could have decided to provide an added entry under the series title (The Foreign and Second Language Educator Series), but in this case chose not to do so.

The card in Figure 2-2 is called a MAIN ENTRY card. In the days when catalog cards were handwritten, catalogers usually prepared only one card with complete bibliographic information. This full card, called the *main entry,* was filed under the author's name, or, when the work had no identifiable author, under the title. Brief or TRUNCATED RECORDS were copied for the subject heading cards and added entries. Now that most catalogers use prepared cards supplied by vendors, however, that distinction between the main entry and other cards no longer applies because all printed cards contain complete information. The term "main entry" now refers to the heading on the top line of the basic card illustrated above. Today this is the heading used to identify the work in bibliographies and other reference books.

VARIATION OF THE RECORD

When an item has no personal author, is the work of a group, or has been produced under editorial direction, the title serves as the main entry and the card is filed by the first word of the title (disregarding the articles: "a," "an," and "the"). To make the title stand out, a variation of form, called HANGING INDENTION, is used. The first line consists of the title, and the other descriptive details are indented below.

```
QB 51
N5        The New astronomy and space science reader /
             ed. by John C. Brandt and Stephen P. Maran.
             -- San Francisco : W. H. Freeman, c1977.
             ix, 371p. : ill. ; 29 cm.
             Bibliography: p. [365] - 367.
             Includes index


             1. Astronomy--Addresses, essays, lectures
          2.  Space sciences--Addresses, essays, lectures
          I.  Brandt, John C.   II. Maran, Stephen P.
```

Figure 2-3

The card in Figure 2-3 is filed under "New," which is capitalized as the filing word. Note that only the spacing varies, and that the same elements of description can be identified.

Figures 2-2 and 2-3 show variations in typed or printed cards. The next four figures show variations between book catalogs, microfilm, and an on-line record. Only the presentation differs, the information remains the same.

Computer-Prepared Book Catalog — Truncated Entries.

MIDDLE GEORGIA REGIONAL LIBRARY – MACON, GEORGIA			NUMBER OF COPIES					
			WASHINGTON	RIVERSIDE	ROCKY CREEK	SHURLING	REGIONAL	MILLEDGEVILLE
Complete Catalog Sequenced By: Author As Of: 05/25/80 Page 2527								
Published by Macon/Bibb County Computer Center.		CALL NUMBER						
Patterson Lillie								
Christmas Feasts And Festivals		J 394.26	3	1	6	3		
Christmas In America		J 394.26	1		1	2	4	
Christmas In Britain And Scandinavia		J 394.26		1	1	1		
Christmas Trick Or Treat By Patterson		JE	1	1	1	1		
Coretta Scott King By Patterson Nc	King Coretta Scott	J 921.	2	1	1	1		
Easter By Patterson		J 394.26	1	1	1	1		
Francis Scott Key Poet And Patriot	Key Francis Scott	J 921.	1	1			2	
Grouchy Santa By Patterson		JE	1	1	1	1		
Halloween		J 394.2	1	3	2	1	2	
Haunted Houses On Halloween By Patterson		JE	1	1	1	1		
Jenny The Halloween Spy By Patterson		JE	1	1	1	1		
Martin Luther King Jr Man Of Peace	King Martin Luther	J 921.		1			1	
Meet Miss Liberty		J 917.471	1					
Sequoyah The Cherokee Who Captured Words	Guess George	J 921.	1		1	1	1	
Patterson Lillie Comp								
Poetry For Spring By Patterson		J 808.81	1	1	1	1	2	

Figure 2-4

Book Catalog Prepared by the Library of Congress

The National Union Catalog

Korella, Karl, 1912–
 Teen-age suicidal gestures; a study of suicidal behavior among high school students. ₁n.p.₁ 1971.
 144 l.
 Thesis (Ph.D.)–University of Oregon.
 Vita.
 Bibliography: leaves 141–144.
 1. Suicide. 2. Adolescence.   I. Title.
 OrU   NUC72–110867

Koreman, J   G   J
 Maastricht in oude ansichten. Door J. G. J. Koreman. Zalthommel, Europese Bibliotheek, 1968.
 160 p. (chiefly illus.) 15 cm. (In oude ansichten) fl 16.90
                                        (Ne 68–24)
 1. Maastricht—Descr.—Views. 1. Title.
 DJ411.M2K6   68–105979
 WU

Koreman, J   G   J
 De stadsrekening van Maastricht over het jaar 1399–1400. ₁Door₁ J. Koreman. Assen, Van Gorcum, 1968.
 156 p. 23 cm. (Maaslandse monografieën, 7) fl 9.90 (fl 8.– pbk)
                                        Ne 68–41
 1. Finance, Public—Maastricht. 2. Maastricht—History—Sources.
 1. Title.
 HJ9510.M3K66   70–378664

Koremblit, Bernardo Ezequiel.
 El ensayo en la Argentina. ₁Buenos Aires Dirección General de Relaciones Culturales, Ministerio de Relaciones Exteriores y Culto, 1964?₁
 29 p. 22 cm.
 1. Argentine essays–Hist. & crit. I. Title.
 CSt MH NIC KU   NUC70–42546

Koren, Edward.
 Don't talk to strange bears. New York, Windmill Books ₁1969₁
 ₁32₁ p. illus. 28 cm. 4.95
 On his walk through the magic woods the little bear follows his mother's warning and does not speak to strange bears, but he speaks to all the other strange animals he meets.
 ₁1. Bears—Stories₁ 1. Title.
 PZ10.3.K83Do   [Fic]   69–16100
 SBN 671–66507–3   MARC

Koren, Emil.
 Tervszerű vasúti pályafenntartási munkáltatási rendszer; a Mérnöki Továbbképző Intézet 1944. évi tanfolyamainak anyaga. Budapest, Egyetemi Nyomda, 1945.
 59 p. illus. 25 cm. (A Mérnöki Továbbképző Intézet kiadványai, M. 62. füzet)
 Cover title.
 1. Railroads—Track. 2. Railroads—Maintenance and repair.
 I. Title.
 TF530.K66   75–292844

Koren, Ephraim.
 The influence of temperature on absorption, translocation and metabolism of pyrazon in sugar beets. ₁Davis, Calif.₁ 1970.
 83 l. illus.
 Thesis–University of California, Davis.
 Typescript.
 CU–A   NUC72–59182

Koren, Eva, 1913–   joint author
 see Marthinsen, Arne. Veileder i praktisk sosialmedisin. 8. omarb. utg. [Oslo] Universitetsforlaget, 1968.

Koren, Eva, 1913–   joint author
 see Strøm, Axel Christian Smith, 1901–
 Veileder i praktisk sosialmedisin. 9. omarb.

Koren, John, 1861–1923, ed.
 The history of statistics, their development and progress in many countries, in memoirs to commemorate the seventy fifth anniversary of The American Statistical Association. New York, B. Franklin ₁1970₁
 xii, 773 p. 23 cm. (Burt Franklin research & source works series, 453. Selected essays in history, economics, and social science, 124)
 Reprint of the 1918 ed.
 Includes bibliographies.
 1. Statistics—History—Addresses, essays, lectures. 1. American Statistical Association. II. Title.
 HA19.K7 1970   310'.9   79–118172
                                        MARC
 KyU

Koren, Karel, ed.
 see V nove čase, Miklavž pri Ormožu, Osnovna šola, 1969.

Koren, Kristian
 see Madshus, Kjell. Cesium-137 in milk in Norway 1962–1966. ₁n.p., 1967?₁

Koren', L   P   1915–
 Есть на Волге утес ... Записки фронтового политработника. Москва, Воениздат, 1969.
 213 p. with illus. 17 cm. (Рассказывают фронтовики) 0.36
                                        USSR 69–VKP
 At head of title: Л. Корень.
 1. Stalingrad, Battle of, 1942–1943—Personal narratives.
 1. Title.
                           Title romanized: Est' na Volge utes.
 D764.3.S7K67   71–531734
 MH NcD CtY CaOTU

Koren, Marvin.
 An optical model study of pion-nucleus and nucleon–nucleus scattering. ₁n.p.₁ 1969.

Figure 2-5

Microfilm Catalog — Subject Entries
Note call numbers at end of entry.

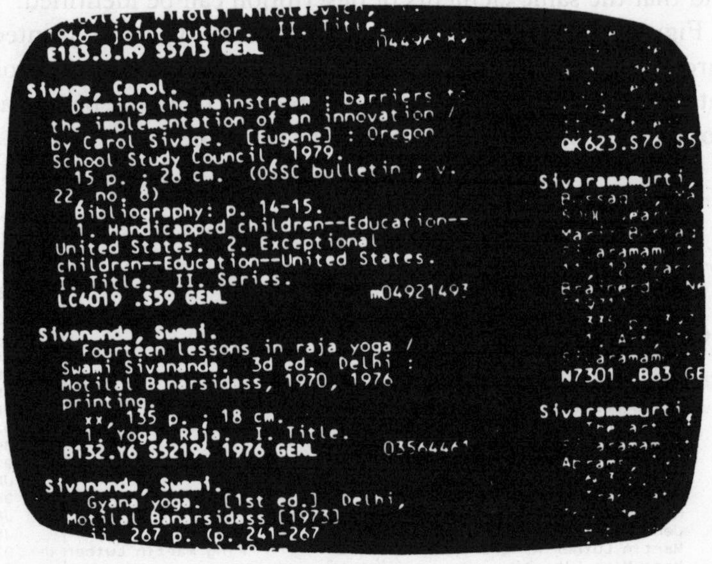

Figure 2-6

On-line Catalog Record (OCLC)

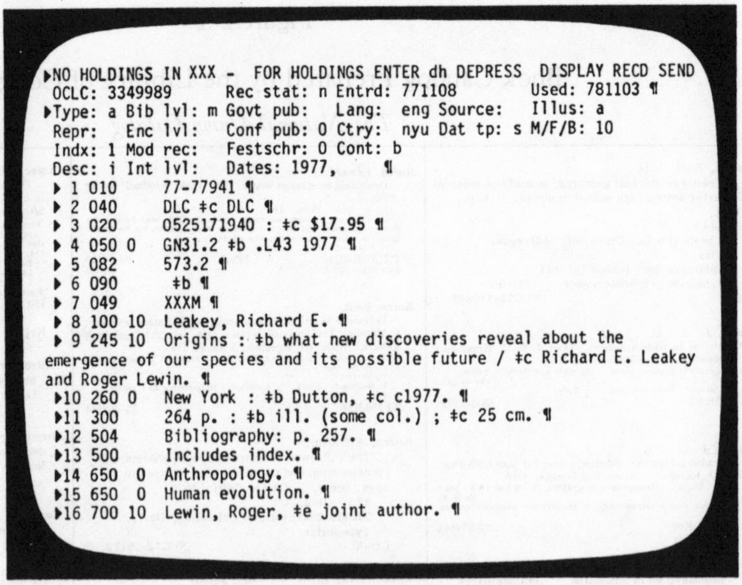

```
▶NO HOLDINGS IN XXX  -  FOR HOLDINGS ENTER dh DEPRESS  DISPLAY RECD SEND
  OCLC: 3349989        Rec stat: n Entrd: 771108        Used: 781103 ¶
▶Type: a Bib lvl: m Govt pub:  Lang: eng Source:  Illus: a
  Repr:    Enc lvl:   Conf pub: 0 Ctry:  nyu Dat tp: s M/F/B: 10
  Indx: 1 Mod rec:    Festschr: 0 Cont: b
  Desc: i Int lvl:    Dates: 1977,      ¶
▶ 1 010       77-77941 ¶
▶ 2 040       DLC ‡c DLC ¶
▶ 3 020       0525171940 : ‡c $17.95 ¶
▶ 4 050 0     GN31.2 ‡b .L43 1977 ¶
▶ 5 082       573.2 ¶
▶ 6 090       ‡b ¶
▶ 7 049       XXXM ¶
▶ 8 100 10    Leakey, Richard E. ¶
▶ 9 245 10    Origins : ‡b what new discoveries reveal about the
  emergence of our species and its possible future / ‡c Richard E. Leakey
  and Roger Lewin. ¶
▶10 260 0     New York : ‡b Dutton, ‡c c1977. ¶
▶11 300       264 p. : ‡b ill. (some col.) ; ‡c 25 cm. ¶
▶12 504       Bibliography: p. 257. ¶
▶13 500       Includes index. ¶
▶14 650 0     Anthropology. ¶
▶15 650 0     Human evolution. ¶
▶16 700 10    Lewin, Roger, ‡e joint author. ¶
```

Figure 2-7

A UNIT RECORD

When the Library of Congress began printing catalog cards
for distribution to libraries it found that the simplest method
was to print only one basic card, containing a complete biblio-

graphic record, and to duplicate this card as needed to make all the entries in a unit. Thus each card, whether main or added entry, is a complete record. Libraries purchased cards in sets and typed headings of their choice in the space above the main entry.

Figure 2-8 shows a UNIT SET. The bibliographic record begins with the author's name as main entry. The cataloger has assigned two additional access points, title and one subject heading, so this unit comprises four cards: author, or main entry card; title, or added entry card; subject card; and shelf list card.

Main Entry—Author

```
   Gibson, Arrell Morgan
      The American Indian : prehistory to the present /
   Arrell Morgan Gibson. -- Lexington, Mass. : D.C.
   Heath, 1980.
      618p. : ill. ; 25 cm.

      Includes bibliographies and index

      1. Indians of North America--History I. Title

E77.G448                        970.004'97        79-84501
                                                      MARC
```

Added Entry—Title Entry

```
   The American Indian

   Gibson, Arrell Morgan
      The American Indian : prehistory to the present /
   Arrell Morgan Gibson. -- Lexington, Mass. : D.C.
   Heath, 1980.
      618p. : ill. ; 25 cm.

      Includes bibliographies and index

      1. Indians of North America--History I. Title

E77.G448                        970.004'97        79-84501
                                                      MARC
```

Figure 2-8

Subject Entry

```
INDIANS OF NORTH AMERICA--HISTORY

Gibson, Arrell Morgan
     The American Indian : prehistory to the present /
Arrell Morgan Gibson. -- Lexington, Mass. : D.C.
Heath, 1980.
     618p. : ill. ; 25 cm.

     Includes bibliographies and index


     1. Indians of North America--History   I. Title
E77.G448                   970.004'97              79-84501
                                                      MARC
```

Shelf List Card

```
Gibson, Arrell Morgan
     The American Indian : prehistory to the present /
Arrell Morgan Gibson. -- Lexington, Mass. : D.C.
Heath, 1980.
     618p. : ill. ; 25 cm.

     12754



     1. Indians of North America--History   I. Title
E77.G448                   970.004'97              79-84501
                                                      MARC
```

Figure 2-8 (continued)

The cards in a unit set are filed alphabetically by whatever appears first at the top of the card, except for the shelf list card. In the example above, Gibson's book about American Indians will be found in the Gs under the author's last name. If the library owns other works by this author these too will be gathered under Gibson. Searches by title, *The American Indian,* will find it in the As. Since the subject is INDIANS OF NORTH AMERICA—HISTORY, it is also filed under that heading, along with all other library materials on that subject.

A shelf list is a catalog arranged for the purpose of taking inventory. It is normally available only to library staff. The shelf list consists of duplicates of the main entry cards with individual designators added. In most cases the designator is the ACCESSION NUMBER, a number assigned to each item as it is acquired. In the example in Figure 2-8 12754 is the accession number; 12753 items were added to the library collection before this book was acquired. The position of the card in the shelf list corresponds to the position of the material on the shelf.

The information for this card was supplied by the Library of Congress. The tracings indicate what headings the LC catalogers added, and recommended call numbers for LCC (E77.G448) or DDC (970.004'97). Additional information includes the order number for this particular card set (79-84501) and MARC indicating that this book has been cataloged on computer tapes of that name. Locally typewritten sets would not include this information.

ORGANIZING THE RECORDS

No matter what the physical form of the catalog, all entries must be arranged in a logical manner. Computer professionals speak of "logical files" and certainly retrieval is difficult unless one understands the system in which records are stored.

Early catalogs were often inventory lists, usually filed in order of acquisition; but catalogers soon experimented with other arrangements. One popular early arrangement by subject, or topic, now known as a CLASSED CATALOG, is unsuitable for author or title searches. When arranged by call numbers, the shelf list resembles a classed catalog because it groups materials by subject.

During the late 19th century the most sophisticated kind of catalog, the DICTIONARY CATALOG, was introduced. In this catalog all entries, whether author, title, or subject, are filed together within a single alphabet. The dictionary catalog offers users complete access to the collection from a single file. It also presents problems, particularly in large collections, where the sheer size and numbers of entries under one term or name can be overwhelming. To alleviate these problems, and to simplify filing, many libraries use a DIVIDED CATALOG. This consists of two files, one for main and added entries, the other for subjects. Both dictionary and divided catalogs exist in the form of cards, books, and microforms.

SUMMARY

Catalog entries consist of standardized records that include elements of information such as author, title, publisher, date, and physical characteristics. These records, or entries about individual items, are gathered together under headings, or access points, so that materials may be seen singly, or as part of a group of works having certain features in common.

Elements are placed on catalog cards in a prescribed and consistent arrangement. This arrangement may alter according to the format of the catalog, but the elements themselves vary only in minor respects. When users become familiar with these bibliographic elements they are more successful in finding information in the catalog.

Entries may be filed in a classed catalog, giving access by subject; in a dictionary catalog, a single file with all entries in alphabetical order; or in a divided catalog, consisting of separate catalogs for subjects, for titles, and for authors.

CHAPTER REVIEW

Terms to understand:

access points	hanging indention
accession numbers	headings
added entries	main entry
classed catalog	MARC
dictionary catalog	omni catalog
divided catalog	tracings
edition	truncated entry
entries	unit set

The catalog record:

Located by headings or access points.

Found under authors, titles, series, other bibliographic details, and standardized subject headings.

One heading — usually author or title — is called the main entry.
Other entries are called added entries.

Unit record — entries are identical except for headings.

Records can be arranged in a single file, the dictionary catalog; in a subject file, the classed catalog; in author, title, and subject files; or in a divided catalog.

CHAPTER 3

CATALOGING CODES: FROM CUTTER TO AACR2

EVERY ITEM in a collection should be identified and described. The basic cataloger's tool for this task is a standard code. Several codes have been written over the years, and, just as the forms of the catalog have changed with technology, so codes have come and gone, each reflecting the information needs of the time in which it was created.

PANIZZI AND CUTTER

The foundations of modern cataloging were laid during the mid-19th century, when the rapid growth of public collections created a need for the organization and classification of books and documents. Early cataloging codes were written with the needs of a particular library in mind, although each built, where it could, upon ideas borrowed from others. One influential code was developed at the British Museum by an Italian refugee, Antonio (later Sir Anthony) Panizzi, who was appointed Keeper of Printed Books in 1837, and Principal Librarian in 1856. Panizzi perceived the importance of a catalog to study and research, and devised a code of 91 rules by which the British Museum catalog, first issued between 1881 and 1900, was created. This pioneering work was continued by an American, Charles Cutter, who served as librarian of the Boston Athenaeum from 1868. Having produced a five-volume catalog of his library, Cutter wrote *Rules for a Printed Dictionary Catalogue* (1875), a code so well formulated that it has influenced modern codes.

In his preface Cutter named three main objectives for a library catalog:

1. To enable a person to find a book of which either is known: author, title, or subject.

2. To show what the library has by a given author, on a given subject, or in a given kind of literature.

3. To assist in the choice of a book: as to its edition (bibliographically), or as to its character (literary or topical).

The catalog, in Cutter's view, should not only identify individual books, but also distinguish between editions, and gather works by the same author, on the same subject, or in the same literary genre. These aims could only be achieved by insuring that new entries were made on the same principles as those already in place. As materials were cataloged, each entry was checked to make sure it was correctly and consistently given. Authors may marry, divorce, add and drop initials, adopt pen names, or otherwise create confusion. Titles may vary from one edition of a work to another and corporate bodies may change their names. Catalogers do not simply record what appears on the title page, but research and assign UNIFORM HEADINGS for authors, corporations, series, and sometimes titles. Many libraries have maintained AUTHORITY FILES, a list of headings already in use, so that catalogers can check every entry before completing the record. By observing these procedures, Cutter's second objective can be attained and the catalog can answer such questions as "How many books do you have by Victoria Holt?" or "Does the American Library Association have a publication about library buildings?"

During the development of a library, however, a number of catalog codes may have been followed and even a small catalog can be difficult to use for this reason. Cutter hoped that codes would provide for "the convenience of the public" by indicating entry choices most likely to be used by the "class of people who use the library." If, following different codes, entries are made under "Clemens, Samuel Langhorn" at one time and under "Twain, Mark" the next; or suddenly switched from place of location to entry under the name of the institution (e.g., "New York. State University," to "State University of New York"), Cutter's hopes for a convenient catalog are dashed.

The lesson to be drawn from this is that the reply, "Look in the catalog," in response to a user's request for assistance is often not a useful answer. Because codes and cataloging rules have changed, even the smallest catalog can be difficult to use.

AFTER CUTTER

By the 1960s cataloging codes, often the complex products of committees, were in urgent need of reexamination. Seymour Lubetzky of the Library of Congress, who was selected for this task, suggested a return to Cutter's principles, and examined existing rules in their light. Lubetzky became the first editor of *Anglo-American Cataloging Rules* (AACR), which were issued in 1967 and generally accepted by British, Canadian, and American libraries. Although AACR1 recognized the growing importance of non-book materials such as filmstrips, the rapid proliferation of new formats and the effect of technology on the form of the catalog soon called for a revised code. *Anglo-American Cataloging Rules, Second Edition* (AACR2), was published in 1978 and formally adopted for international use in 1981.

When AACR1 was published, it was predicted to be the last code written for the card form of a catalog, and this has indeed been the case. Use of the card catalog has declined as more and more information has been stored in computer data bases and transmitted to users by terminals or on microform. Even the terminology of cataloging has changed. Access is gained to a data base via an access point, not through main or added entries, and whereas earlier codes discussed "Choice of Entry," AACR2 contains a chapter called "Choice of Access Points."

Cataloging practice has not only been changed by the computer, but also by an increase in the number of non-book formats acquired by libraries, such as video tapes, games, kits, and computer discs as well as books, films, and recordings. This innovation has had an especially pronounced effect on school libraries, many of which have been renamed "media centers." Among the cataloging difficulties presented by these new materials is the problem of assigning an author entry to items such as films that are created by several people. Main entry under title has therefore become more common in the present code, and the term author has been more strictly defined.

During the 1960s rapid progress was made in establishing international cataloging standards. A group representing major nations and languages that met in Paris in 1961 formulated guidelines called the Paris Principles, which were prefaced, like Cutter's rules, by a statement of the functions of the catalog. Descriptive cataloging was reformed by the publication of *International Standard Bibliographic Description* (ISBD) in 1974. This was an international format for description of books that could be understood and filed into the catalogs of other countries and converted into machine-readable form. Rules for other forms of material were promised. If cataloging was to reflect international practice it needed to be incorporated in the code.

During this same period North American publishers began

to assign an individual number to each edition of a work. The *International Standard Book Number* (ISBN) and the *International Standard Serial Number* (ISSN) are now routinely printed on title pages or some prominent place in most books, magazines, and a growing number of other types of materials. These numbers (see Figure 3-1) provide another means of identifying and accessing individual titles.

AACR2, edited by Paul Winkler and Michael Gorman (Gorman also edited *The Concise AACR2*, 1981) takes these many forces into account and brings local practices up to date. These rules proposed many changes in cataloging practice, and were not adopted without controversy.

AACR2

The code is divided into two parts, corresponding to the two basic purposes of the catalog. Part I, DESCRIPTION, states the rules for bibliographic and physical description and is based on the ISBD formats. Part II, HEADINGS, UNIFORM TITLES AND REFERENCES, provides guidance in the choice of headings and access points, and is based on the 1961 Paris Principles. This organization follows the order in which catalogers work. In Part I, the cataloger will find guidance for describing the item in hand and prepares that part of the card shaded in Figure 3-1. (Note addition of the ISBN in the note area.)

```
Comanor, William S.
    Advertising and market power / William S. Comanor
and Thomas A. Wilson. -- Cambridge, Mass. : Harvard
University Press, 1974.
    xvi., 257p. : ill. ; 25cm. -- (Harvard economic
studies ; v. 144)
    Includes bibliographical references and index
    ISBN 0-674-00580-5


    1. Advertising   I. Wilson, Thomas Arthur, 1935-
joint author   II. Title   III. Series

HF5827.C587                 659.1            73-90849
Library of Congress         74 [4]           MARC
```

Figure 3-1

Part II provides rules for the selection of headings and access points, given in those portions of the card that are shaded in Figure 3-2.

```
Comanor, William S.
    Advertising and market power / William S. Comanor
and Thomas A. Wilson. -- Cambridge, Mass. : Harvard
University Press, 1974.
    xvi., 257p. : ill. ; 25cm. -- (Harvard economic
studies ; v. 144)
    Includes bibliographical references and index
    ISBN 0-674-00580-5


    1. Advertising  I. Wilson, Thomas Arthur, 1935-
joint author  II. Title  III. Series
HF5827.C587                659.1          73-90849
Library of Congress         74 [4]           MARC
```

Figure 3-2

The editors of AACR2 anticipated that the appearance of new formats after the publication of their book would create a need for more rules and they left chapters 14 through 20 blank to accommodate them. AACR2 contains rules for the description of books, cartographic materials, manuscripts, music, sound recordings, motion pictures and video recordings, graphic materials (including filmstrips), machine-readable data files, three-dimensional artifacts and realia, microforms, and serials. Although their aim is to standardize cataloging procedures, the editors recognize that "uniform legislation for all types and sizes of catalogues is neither possible nor desirable," and encourage "the application of individual judgement based on specific local knowledge." It is necessary for the cataloger to develop a sense of local priorities in order to make appropriate cataloging decisions.

SUMMARY

Cataloging codes are important because they determine the structure of the catalog and, ultimately, the users' success in retrieving information. Following a standard code also makes it possible for libraries to share materials and allows patrons to use the catalog of any library. In 1876 Charles Cutter identified two major purposes of the catalog: to locate an individual work, and to gather, or relate works that share bibliographic characteristics. Librarians still try to achieve Cutter's objectives. Today, librarians are called upon to catalog all manner of items from collections of geological specimens to rare books, and to provide bibliographic information that can be internationally understood. AACR2 was developed in the effort to meet such challenges.

CHAPTER REVIEW

Terms to understand:

Anglo-American Cataloging Rules, 2nd ed. (AACR2)
Authority File
International Standard Bibliographic Description (ISBD)
International Standard Book Number (ISBN)
International Standard Serial Number (ISSN)

Purpose of the catalog:

To enable a person to find a book of which either author, title, or subject is known.
To show what the library has by a given author, on a given subject, in a given kind of literature.
To assist in the choice of a book.

AACR2 provides:

ISBN punctuation
Cataloging rules for various formats, including rules for describing materials and assigning access points.

CHAPTER 4

DESCRIBING THE ITEM: AACR2 PART I

DESCRIPTIVE CATALOGING has become more multifarious as formats have proliferated. Part I of AACR2, entitled "Description," provides rules for this part of the cataloging process.

CONCEPTS OF DESCRIPTION

Rules for description are based on five principles:

a) The elements of description
b) Punctuation
c) Sources of information
d) Levels of description
e) Standard terminology

The description of an item is divided into eight areas, known as the elements of description:

Title and statement of responsibility
Edition
*Material (or type of publication) specific details
Publication, distribution, etc.
Physical description
Series
Notes
Standard number and terms of availability

*(Applicable only to cartographic materials and serials.)

THE ELEMENTS OF DESCRIPTION

Except for the addition of the standard number (ISBN), these are the elements catalogers have normally recorded in the past. When library materials consisted primarily of books, however, the publication and distribution area was known as the imprint and the physical description area as the collation. To prepare an entry these elements are first located and identified in the item being cataloged.

PUNCTUATION

The current system of punctuation (ISBD) is an international creation, developed to assist the conversion of cataloging information into machine readable form. Use of this punctuation and sequence makes it possible to identify each element as it appears in the descriptive record even when the language in which the entry is written is not known to the cataloger.

Although ISBD punctuation may look strange to the uninitiated, it is relatively easy to master. The eight elements are separated by a full stop, indicated by a period, a space, and an em dash (—). Because most typewriters do not have an em dash, use two hyphens instead (--). Unless starting a new paragraph, separate all elements of the description by full stops.

Other punctuation may be required within elements, and this is demonstrated as each is discussed.

SOURCES OF
INFORMATION

Catalogers should not only follow common principles in recording elements, they should also derive their information from the same parts of the materials. If one cataloger consults the book jacket or the filmstrip box, whereas another uses the book's title page or the label on the film can, they are unlikely to produce identical descriptions. When cataloging books one turns first to the title and copyright pages, where bibliographic information will be found. The title page is now a standard convention, with certain information routinely printed on the back (verso) as well as the front of that page. This is not the case in many other formats, such as games or realia, which have no comparable convention. The code gives catalogers a standard to use by identifying a Chief Source of Information for each format, along with acceptable secondary sources. The Chief Source of Information is the first place to look when preparing to record the elements of description.

LEVELS OF
DESCRIPTION

Early catalog codes were created primarily for use in large collections where it was assumed that readers were interested in full bibliographic description. Printed Library of Congress cards follow this practice. Because many libraries do not need complete descriptive details, there is a demand for "short," "medium," and "full" cataloging that is supplied to some extent by commercial vendors of simplified cataloging copy. AACR2 was the first widely accepted code to recognize this need.

AACR2 allows a choice among three levels of description; from First Level, the minimum amount of information, to Third Level, the most detailed. In some libraries, it is sufficient to record the number of pages or type of film. Others include not only the number of pages, but the height of the book; not only the type of film, but also the running time. AACR2 encourages catalogers to make decisions about the level of description according to the information needs of users.

As formats have multiplied it has become necessary to tell users whether a work such as *Hamlet* takes the form of a film, a video tape, a sound recording, or a printed text. To insure that the terms used to describe these formats do not vary AACR2 provides standard terminology.

Some libraries maintain a separate catalog for each format, others list all materials in an omni catalog. For users of omni catalogs AACR2 provides the option of a GENERAL MATERIALS DESIGNATION [GMD], which is given in brackets immediately after the title proper. The GMD alerts users to the general physical class to which an item belongs; e.g., Christmas concertos [sound recording]; The Search for solutions [motion picture]. When a library decides to use this option the cataloger selects the correct term from either the British or the American list (see Figure 4-1). These general terms are further clarified in the physical description area of the record.

These five principles are important in the construction of a bibliographic record. The elements of description are areas included in an entry, appearing in a prescribed order. ISBD punctuation highlights each of these elements, and Sources of Information determine where one looks for them on the item being cataloged. Standard terminology insures that the various formats will be referred to in consistent terms.

CONSTRUCTING THE ENTRY

The cataloger cannot construct an entry until format, Chief Source of Information, and level of description have been determined. These steps follow in logical order.

Step One	Determine the format and the Chief Source of Information for the item being cataloged.
Step Two	Determine the level of description to be given.
Step Three	Identify and record the descriptive elements as they are to appear in the completed entry.

Step One. *Determine the format of the item, and the Chief Source of Information.*

The cataloger first decides what type of material is being cataloged and which rules apply. There are rules for description of the following formats:

books, pamphlets, and printed sheets
cartographic materials

manuscripts
music
sound recordings
motion pictures and video-recordings
graphic materials (including filmstrips and photos)
machine-readable data files
microforms
serials

In most cases, decisions about format are easily made, and only multimedia sets present difficulties. The kind of format determines the Chief Source of Information.

Once the format of the material is decided, the cataloger examines the correct sources of information on that item. This is an important step, because it is possible for items to have one title on the spine or jacket, and another on a label, or for dates and names to vary. Figure 4-2 lays out the sources of information for each format.

The initial examination is often called TECHNICAL READING. This is not a full reading or viewing, but a process of identifying the pieces of information that make up the elements of description for the item in hand. The Chief Source of Information is the first place to look, and if the technical reading reveals that titles or dates differ within an item then the information in the Chief Source should be followed.

Information on the item itself frequently differs from that on the package or accompanying material. For example, a sound recording may have one title on the jacket and another on the label. In this case the title on the label (the Chief Source of Information for sound recordings) is the title used by the cataloger for the catalog record.

When the Chief Source is missing, or is inadequate, the other sources are consulted in descending order. According to the chart the Chief Source of Information for a microfilm is the title frame. If no title frame exists, accept information from the following places: 1) the rest of the item 2) the container 3) accompanying printed materials or 4) another source. Often details such as dates are not given on the sound recording label, but can be identified somewhere on the jacket. Thus, when no date exists on the Chief Source, take any date found on other acceptable sources. In general, information found on the item itself should be preferred to information given elsewhere, either in accompanying material or on the packaging. Only rarely do catalogers supply details, and these are always clearly distinguished by enclosing them in brackets.

GENERAL MATERIALS DESIGNATIONS

British Terms	North American Terms
cartographic material	map
	globe
graphic	art original
	chart
	filmstrip
	flash card
	picture
	slide
	technical drawing
	transparency
machine-readable data file	machine-readable data file
manuscript	manuscript
microform	microform
motion picture	motion picture
multimedia	kit
music	music
object	diorama
	game
	microscope slide
	model
	realia
sound recording	sound recording
text	text
videorecording	videorecording

Figure 4-1

Step Two. *Determine the level of description.*

The level of description determines which descriptive details will appear in the final record. Not all items in a collection may need records of equal detail and libraries need not adopt one level or another consistently. A library can choose a level and describe all materials by this standard. Others may decide on the level of detail according to the nature of the item being cataloged, and the information needs of those most likely to use it.

For First Level of Description, include at least the basic elements with a few additional details. Observe the full stop between each element, and the other punctuation used within each area.

First Level
of Description

1st
paragraph

Title proper / first statement of responsibility, if different from main entry head-

31

SOURCES OF INFORMATION

Where to look for Descriptive Elements	BOOKS, PAMPHLETS, AND PRINTED SHEETS	CARTOGRAPHIC MATERIALS
CHIEF SOURCE OF INFORMATION	Title page	A) Cartographic item, itself B) Container or case, cradle and stand
Alternative Sources	If no chief source, take that part of the item that supplies the most information. (Cover, half-title page, colophon, etc.)	If information is not available from the chief source take it from any accompanying material.

Where to look for Descriptive Elements	MUSIC	SOUND RECORDINGS
CHIEF SOURCE OF INFORMATION	Use as the chief source whichever of the "list" title page, the cover, or the caption furnishes the fullest information.	TYPE — CHIEF SOURCE Disc — Label (attached to disc) Tape (open reel-to-reel) — Reel and label Tape cassette — Cassette and label Tape cartridge — Cartridge and label Roll — Label Sound recording on film — Container and label Treat accompanying textual material on a container as the chief source if it supplies a collective title, and the parts do not.
Alternative Sources	If no chief source, take from the following (in order of preference): caption cover colophon other preliminaries or other sources	

Where to look for Descriptive Elements	MOTION PICTURES AND VIDEO RECORDINGS	GRAPHIC MATERIALS
CHIEF SOURCE OF INFORMATION	The film itself (e.g., the title frames) and its container (and its label) if the container is an integral part of the item (e.g., a cassette).	The item itself including any labels permanently affixed and a container that is an integral part. If of two or more physical parts, treat the container that is the unifying element as the chief source if it supplies a collective title.
Alternative Sources	If no chief source, take from the following (in order of preference): accompanying textual material (e.g., scripts, short lists, publicity items)	If no chief source, take from the following (in order of preference): container (box, frame, etc.) accompanying textual material (manuals, leaflets) other sources

SOURCES OF INFORMATION

Where to look for Descriptive Elements	MACHINE-READABLE DATA FILES	THREE-DIMENSIONAL ARTIFACTS AND REALIA
CHIEF SOURCE OF INFORMATION	The internal user label, when it is adequate. If no user label, take from the following (in order of preference): documentation issued by creator of the file other published description of file other sources (including the container)	The object itself, together with any accompanying textual material and container issued by publisher or manufacturer of item.
Alternative Sources		Prefer information found on the object itself (including affixed labels) to information found in accompanying textual material or on the container.

Where to look for Descriptive Elements	MICROFORMS		SERIALS
CHIEF SOURCE OF INFORMATION	TYPE	CHIEF SOURCE	The title page of the first issue or the first issue that is available.
	Microfilm	Title frame	If no chief source, take from the following (in order of preference): cover caption masthead editorial pages colophon other pages
	Aperture cards	Case for the set, the title card, or if a single card; the card itself	
	Microfiche and Micro-opaques	Title frame	
	If information is presented on successive frames or cards, treat these all as the chief source.		
Alternative Source	If no chief source, take from the following (in order of preference): rest of the item, including container container accompanying printed material any other source		If information traditionally given on the title pages is given on facing pages, treat the two pages as the title page.

Figure 4-2

ing in form or number or if there is no main entry heading. — Edition statement. — Material (or type of publication) specific detail. First publisher, etc., date of publication, etc.

2nd paragraph	Extent of item
3rd paragraph	Note(s)
Above Tracing	Standard number

Note that the first statement of responsibility should be omitted when it is identical to the main entry at the head of the record. Place of publication and series information are also omitted. When these details are considered important they can be included in the First Level. For instance, place of publication might be omitted as a general rule, but included when the publisher is a local company.

Second Level of Description

The Second Level of Description includes more details. Statements of responsibility are expanded to include all those with creative responsibility mentioned in the Chief Source of Information, for example: translators, editors, and illustrators. Place of publication is included and the physical details are augmented with dimensions and other data concerning the appearance of the item. Series information is fully given. The record becomes longer and more definite.

1st paragraph	Title proper [general material designation]
	= parallel title : other title information / first statement of responsibility ; each subsequent statement of responsibility
	— edition statement / first statement of responsibility relating to the edition
	— material (or type of publication) specific details (for cartographic materials and serials)
	— first place of publication, etc. : first publishers, etc., date of publication, etc.
2nd paragraph	Extent of item : other physical details ; dimensions

	— (Title proper of series / statement of responsibility relating to series, ISSN of series ; numbering within the series. Title of subseries, ISSN of subseries ; numbering within subseries)
3rd paragraph	Note(s)
Above Tracing	Standard number

Note the punctuation used within each element. A slash separates title information from statements of responsibility. Colons separate places from publishers, and series information is put in parentheses. As noted, use of the GMD is optional, and usually is determined by the library's cataloging policy.

The Third Level of Description is usually lengthy because it includes all elements that are applicable. Nothing is omitted: names associated with the work, publishers, distributors, series information, and physical details are included, whether considered essential information or not.

Third Level of Description

How does the cataloger select an appropriate level? If a library draws up guidelines for the use of all three levels, these points should be taken into consideration.

CHOOSING APPROPRIATE DESCRIPTIVE LEVELS

1. The information needs of library users. For example, place of publication is often required for students preparing bibliographies and can be added to First Level although it would ordinarily be omitted.

2. The availability of staff and other resources for cataloging activities. When the staff has little time for cataloging, First Level provides a basic standard description and meets the needs of those searching for popular reading materials. On those rare occasions when a missing bibliographic detail is needed, a common reference tool can supply it. Those libraries that catalog by format rather than producing a single omni catalog may elect to use First Level.

3. The nature of materials being added to the collection. Locally produced or published materials are not likely to be listed in standard reference tools, nor found on the shelves of every library. Such material should be described in detail, for the cataloging record may be the only record of that item in existence. These items, as well as rare or valuable mate-

rials, should be cataloged at Level Two or Level Three. The chart in Figure 4-4 offers suggestions for deciding levels of description.

Step Three. *Identify and record the descriptive elements as they appear in the final record.*

After the level of description has been selected the cataloger identifies and records the desired elements found in the technical reading. Most of these elements are given in the Chief Source of Information. When giving a book a technical reading, examine the verso of the title page carefully.

LEVELS OF CATALOGING

```
Davidson, Audrey
    Substance and manner -- Hiawatha Press,
1977.
    130p.

    Includes bibliographical references


    ISBN 0-930276-01-9
```

Level One

```
Davidson, Audrey
    Substance and manner : studies in music
and the other arts / by Audrey Davidson ;
pref. by Herbert M. Scheuller. -- St. Paul,
Minn. : Hiawatha Press, 1977.
    xii, 103 p. : music ; 23 cm.
    Includes bibliographical references


    ISBN 0-930276-01-9
```

Level Two

Figure 4-3

Since the mid-1970s Cataloging in Publication data (CIP) has been printed on the verso of the title page. CIP is an incomplete cataloging record supplied by the Library of Congress before a book is printed. It helps establish the main entry, identifies the title, and indicates notes. Always take note of this information during the technical reading.

Cataloging in Publication

FIRST LEVEL	• Accept First Level description given in prepared cataloging copy purchased by the library. • When staffing is inadequate, use First Level for most cataloging produced in the library. • Consider using First Level for materials listed in common bibliographic tools. • Consider using First Level for materials included in common reference indexing tools. • Consider using First Level for fiction and juvenile titles requiring limited retrieval information: mysteries, romances, science fiction, and westerns.
SECOND LEVEL	• Accept Second Level description given in prepared cataloging copy purchased by the library. • Use at least Second Level for items of particular importance; e.g., a special collection of materials of local interest. • Use at least Second Level when it is important to include elements that distinguish one format from another; e.g., all versions of *Oliver Twist*

THIRD LEVEL	• Always use Third Level when materials have a special local significance:
	    Locally published genealogies.
	    Locally produced materials added to the permanent collection.
	    Publications of local significance not likely to be included in standard bibliographic tools or reference sources.
	    Local oral histories.
	• Use Third Level for any rare or valuable item.

Figure 4-4

DESCRIBING AND RECORDING DESCRIPTIVE ELEMENTS

A title is essential at any level of description and catalogers have characterized and defined the various types.

Title and Statement of Responsibility

Title Proper — the chief name for a work, including an alternative title, but excluding other types of title information.

Alternative Title — the second part of a title proper, consisting of two parts joined by "or"

The tempest, or, the enchanted island

Marcel Marceau, ou, L'art du mime

Parallel Title — the title proper in another language. Parallel titles are preceded by the = sign.

To catch a mongoose = Pour attraper une mangouste

Other Title Information — A sub-title that further amplifies the meaning of the title proper. Colons preceded and followed by a space separate the title proper from other title information.

Africa : adventure in eyewitness history

Collective Title — A title proper that is an inclusive title for an item containing several works. Collective titles may be taken from any source of information. When a collective title is used, the individual content titles may be listed in the notes area.

Pete Seeger's children's concert

Supplied Title — A brief descriptive title supplied by the cataloger when no title is found. Always enclosed in brackets [   ].

To record, transcribe the title proper exactly as it appears, capitalizing only proper names. Some punctuation may be altered, or replaced, with a dash. Include apostrophes and commas as given. Record the periods used to denote initials or abbreviations, but omit the space that in normal usage

ITEM	TITLE	SOURCE OF INFORMATION	TITLE PROPER AS RECORDED
book	F.B.I. In Peace and War	title page	F.B.I. in peace and war
film loop	Lettering For Projection	label on container	Lettering for projection
sound recording	Kindergarten Songs Kindergarten Album I	on jacket on label	Kindergarten album I
videotape	untitled boxing match	cataloger	[Ali-Holmes heavyweight title fight, 1980]
book	Guidelines Regarding Individuals Responsible For Continued Professional Development Program For Teachers in Local Education Agencies	title page	Guidelines regarding individuals responsible for continued professional development...

follows a period to avoid confusing these with the full stops used in ISBD punctuation. A lengthy title may be shortened after the first five words, provided that no essential information is omitted. Indicate omissions with ellipses (...). When there is no given title, supply an appropriate one and enclose this in brackets.

Use of the GMD, an option provided by AACR2, is recommended for those libraries that collect many types of materials and enter everything in an omni catalog. In order to alert the user to the general format of the item, place the GMD directly after title proper, separating it from other parts of the title. Only alternative titles are not affected. When this option is taken always select the GMD from the appropriate list, British or American (See Figure 4-2). Be consistent in both terminology and form.

Recording the General Materials Designations

Alternative title	Marcel Marceau, ou, L'art du mime [text]
Parallel title	To catch a mongoose [text] = Pour attraper une mangouste
Sub-title	Africa [text] : adventure in eyewitness history
Supplied title	[Ali-Holmes heavyweight title fight, 1980] [videorecording]

Sub-titles may be omitted with First Level. However, they often provide a fuller explanation of the work and are especially important when the title proper is uninformative about the content. *Belly to belly, back to back*, for instance, is about "the militant humanism of Robert R. Carkhoff," as its sub-title indicates. Users will not recognize this work for what it is unless the sub-title is included.

Other Title Information

To add sub-titles or parallel titles to a First Level description, place them (with proper punctuation) either in the first paragraph, or first in the notes area.

Second and Third Level description contains all title information. Note that Other Title Information is preceded by a space, colon, space (:). Parallel titles are distinguished by the equal sign (=).

First Level   Belly to belly, back to back /

Notes for First Level	Subtitle: The militant humanism of Robert R. Carkhoff
Second Level	Belly to belly, back to back [text] : the militant humanism of Robert R. Carkhoff /

Statements of Responsibility

The Chief Source of Information normally indicates who wrote, sang, illustrated, or otherwise participated in the item's creation. This information, the statement of responsibility, is transcribed immediately after the title information and separated from it by a slash. First Level suggests recording such a statement only when it differs from the main entry. Second Level includes all prominent names, while Third Level lists all those responsible for the work. List these names in the order in which they appear, taking the form of the name as given, but omitting titles unless they are an integral part of the name (e.g., Dr. Seuss). Transcribe exactly as given in the Chief Source of Information including verbs describing participation, such as illustrated, edited, or written. If no such verbs appear they should not be added unless absolutely necessary for clarity, in which case enclose them in brackets, e.g., [drawings by]. If four or more people perform the same function (e.g., author) omit all but the first person listed. Explanatory notes or phrases may be added if the relationship between the work and the person is not clear.

Chief Source of Information (Title page)	Dive! the Story of an Atomic Submarine Commander H. B. Harris-Warren, U.S.M.
First Level	Dive! [text]
Second Level	Dive! [text] : the story of an atomic submarine / H. B. Harris-Warren. — New York
Chief Source of Information (Record label)	The fall of the House of Usher and other tales by Edgar Allen Poe read by Vincent Price.
First Level	The fall of the House of Usher [sound recording]
Second Level	The fall of the House of Usher [sound recording] : and other tales / by Edgar Allen Poe; read by Vincent Price. —

Chief Source of Information (Title page)	Teaching Mathematics, Psychological Foundations
	    F. Joe Crosswhite
	    John L. Higgins
	    Alan R. Osborne
	    Richard J. Shumway

First Level	Teaching mathematics / F. Joe Crosswhite . . . [et al.]. —
Second Level	Teaching mathematics [text] : psychological foundations / F. Joe Crosswhite . . . [et al.]. —

An edition consists of all copies of an item produced from the master copy. Subsequent editions may make substantial changes in the original content; thus, catalogers treat editions as distinct works. When edition information is found in the Chief Source of Information, it is recorded following the statement of responsibility. Use standard abbreviations (see appendix) and arabic numbers in place of words; i.e., 3rd, not third. In Second and Third Levels also include any statements of responsibility related to a new edition, such as the editor who prepared the revision.

Edition Area

Chief Source of Information (title page)	A Dictionary of Modern English Usage by H. W. Fowler Second Edition revised by Sir Ernest Gowers
First Level	A dictionary of modern English usage — 2nd ed. —
Second Level	A dictionary of modern English usage / by H. W. Fowler. — 2nd ed. / rev. by Ernest Gowers. —

The area of publication includes the names of all publishers, distributors, or agencies responsible for making the item available. For all levels, these names are listed in the order in which they appear in the Chief Source of Information. First Level omits place of publication; all levels include a publication or production date. Transcribe the name of the town or city as it appears, unless addition of a larger geographical unit aids identification (e.g., Garden City, N.J.). Use a space, colon, and space (:) between the place and the name of the agency, and abbreviate the name to the shortest form by which

Publication and Distribution Area

41

it can be recognized. Generalities such as "Company" or "Ltd." are entirely omitted. Use the most recent date given in the Chief Source of Information, unless there is a wide variance between publication and copyright dates. When this occurs, make it known by including both. For non-book materials, it is always important to consult the Chief Source of Information for the original date of production. Many older copyrighted materials have been reissued and this is not always apparent on the new packaging. Supply an approximate date when no date is given and enclose this in brackets.

Chief Source of Information	As recorded
no date given, but probably produced in the 1970s	, [197-]. —
McGraw-Hill Book Company	: McGraw-Hill,
The Oryx Press in Phoenix	. — Phoenix [Ariz.] : Oryx Press,
1979 publication date on the package, 1967 copyright date on the title frame	, 1979, c1967. —
Published by Western Publishing Company, New York. Developed by Academic Games Associates, Inc.	. — New York : Western Publishing ; developed by Academic Games Assoc, 1969. —

Those publishers who have offices in several cities usually list all of them. The cataloger need only name the first; e.g., R. R. Bowker Company, New York and London. — New York : Bowker. If the first named city is not in the home country of the cataloger, however, both can be recorded. A cataloger in England would record the above as: — New York; London : Bowker.

Physical Description Area

For the physical description area the cataloger will rely on a technical reading to answer these four questions:

What is the extent of the item?
What are its other physical details?
What are its dimensions?
Does it come with accompanying materials?

Formerly, users could assume that whatever physical details were supplied, they applied to a book. Now it is necessary to record descriptions of all available formats according to a prescribed method.

The GMD alerts users to the general form in which the content is packaged, such as a sound recording, but whether this sound recording is on cartridge, cassette, disc, or tape should also be noted. This specific indication of format is supplied in the Physical Description Area with the SPECIFIC MATERIAL DESIGNATION. Whereas inclusion of the GMD is optional, recording the specific material designation is obligatory. Figure 4-5 relates the list of [GMD] terms to the more specific terms used in this area. These terms are used exclusively because formats and the terms used to describe them have proliferated. For example, Library of Congress has been cataloging "phonorecords" for years, while others have cataloged "sound discs" or "audio recordings." Terminology has even varied within catalogs.

Begin a new paragraph and record the extent of the item, using arabic numerals, standard terminology taken from the chart, and standard abbreviations (See appendix). For First Level, only the extent of the item need be recorded. Second and Third Levels require more extensive detail:

Specific material designation (if other than a book)

Size in number of pages, volumes, frames, length, or other suitable unit of measure

Presence of illustrations, use of color ; dimensions, diameter, playing speed, etc.

Accompanying materials

The extent of the item is separated from other details by a space, colon, space (:) and accompanying material should be indicated with a plus sign (+). Figure 4-6 illustrates First and Second Level physical description for the various formats. Note the punctuation and types of details included for each.

A series title is a collective title applied to a group of separate items, each of which has its own title. Although series information has nothing to do with physical description, it immediately follows this area, in the same paragraph. Series details are enclosed in parentheses, recorded and punctuated in the same manner as the title proper.

Series Area

Series are usually PUBLISHER SERIES, that is, a publisher commissioned a number of authors to write individual works under a collective title. Examples include the *Rivers of Amer-*

SPECIFIC MATERIAL DESCRIPTIONS

CLASS OF MATERIALS	GMD (List 2)	SPECIFIC MATERIALS DESIGNATIONS	
Books, Pamphlets, and Printed Sheets	Text	Number of pages or leaves in accordance with the terminology suggested by the volume.	
Cartographic Materials	Map Globe	aerial chart aerial remote sensing image anamorphic map atlas bird's-eye view or map view block diagram celestial chart celestial globe chart hydrographic chart imaginative map map map profile	map section orthophoto photo mosaic (controlled) photo mosaic (uncontrolled) photomap plan relief model remote-sensing image space remote-sensing image terrestrial remote-sensing image topographic drawing topographic print
Manuscripts	Manuscript	Record sequences of leaves or pages.	
Music	Music	score condensed score close score miniature score piano (violin, etc.) conductor part	vocal score piano score chorus score part
		If none of the terms above is appropriate, use v. of music or leaves of music. If a manuscript, add ms. to the term.	
Sound recordings	Sound recording	sound cartridge sound cassette sound disc	sound tape reel sound track film
		Use terms piano roll, organ roll, etc. as appropriate for rolls. If GMD is used, drop the word sound from all the above, except the last.	
Motion pictures and videorecordings	Motion picture Videorecording	film cartridge film cassette film loop film reel	videocartridge videocassette videodisc videoreel

If GMD is used, drop film or video from all the above terms.

CLASS OF MATERIALS	GMD (List 2)	SPECIFIC MATERIALS DESIGNATIONS		
Graphic Materials	Art original Chart Filmstrip Flash card Picture Slide Technical drawing Transparency	art original art print art reproduction chart filmslip filmstrip flash card flip chart	photograph picture postcard poster radiograph slide stereograph study print	technical drawing transparency wall chart
		Add to filmstrip and stereograph the words cartridge or reel as appropriate.		
Machine-readable data files	Machine-readable data files	data file program file object program		
		Add in parentheses to the designation for a data file the number of logical records. Add in parentheses to the designation for a program file the number of statements and the name of the programming language.		
Artifacts and realia	Diorama Game Microscope slide Model Realia	diorama exhibit game microscope slide	mock-up model	
		If none of these terms is appropriate, give the specific name of the item as concisely as possible, (e.g., hand puppet, quilt, etc.)		
Microforms	Microform	aperture card microfiche	microfilm micro-opaque	
		If the GMD is used, drop the prefix micro for these terms. Add cartridge, cassette, or reel as appropriate.		
Serials	no GMD	Give the relevant specific material designation for the class of material to which the item belongs, (e.g., wall chart, filmstrip, v., microfiche, etc.)		

Figure 4-5

45

EXAMPLES OF FIRST AND SECOND LEVEL PHYSICAL DESCRIPTIONS

	FIRST LEVEL	SECOND LEVEL
BOOKS	231p. (last arabic numbered page is 231) 3v. (the book is in three volumes)	231p. : ill., charts, 13 cm. 3v. : ports., 17 cm. Use ill. for all illustrated materials. If the book also contains charts, coats of arms, facsimiles, forms, genealogical tables, maps, music, plans, portraits, samples, indicate with term or its abbreviation.
SOUND RECORDINGS	1 sound disc 2 sound cassettes	1 sound disc (30 min.) : 33-1/3 rpm, stereo, 12 in. + pamphlet 2 sound cassettes (80 min.) : 3¾ ips, stereo The physical description is provided for the user's information. For example, it is likely the user will want to know how long a sound recording plays, at what speed, number of sound channels, and if there is accompanying material.
MOTION PICTURES AND VIDEORECORDINGS	1 film cassette 1 video cassette	1 film cassette (25 min.) : sd., col., super 8 mm. 1 videocassette (38 min.) : sil, B&W, ½ in.
ARTIFACTS AND REALIA	1 game 1 metric ruler	1 game : (board, cards, 6 tokens, 2 dice) + instructions 1 metric ruler : in box 25x8x3 cm. + manual
FILMSTRIPS	1 filmstrip 4 filmstrips	1 filmstrip (24 fr.) : col. ; 35 mm. 4 filmstrips : sd., col. ; 35 mm. + 2 sound cassettes + 1 instructional guide.
SLIDES	12 slides	12 slides : col. + 1 teacher's manual

Figure 4-6

ica, the *I Can Read* series, and *The American Poets* series of filmstrips. More rare are AUTHOR'S SERIES, in which all the titles are written by the same person, as in *The Story of Civilization* by Will and Ariel Durant. Some materials are better known by their series name than by individual titles and this is particularly true of educational materials, such as textbook series.

Although First Level omits series information entirely, libraries that choose this level of description may wish to include series information and provide access points for a series title familiar to users. This decision should be based on the anticipated needs of those who are likely to use the item being cataloged.

When using Second Level, record series information in full, providing statements of responsibility for a series editor, and include the ISSN number when given. Numbering within the series is recorded with standard abbreviations and arabic numerals.

- (Family Library of Great Music)
- (Harvard East Asian series; 79)
- (University of Toronto, Dept. of English. Studies and Texts No. 37)
- (The Pocketbook library of great art)

If series information is not clearly identified as such, omit it.

Not all catalog records contain notes. Typed and computerized records often omit them. Notes, however, provide information that is not easily given elsewhere. AACR2 describes 21 varieties of notes from which the cataloger can choose. Common types of notes include: page numbers of bibliographies; information about other editions of the work; lists of accompanying materials; intended audience or reading levels; a summary or list of contents; and other formats in which the content appears. For instance, school media centers may choose to include reading levels in the notes area. Annotations are often given for juvenile works, or for materials that are not easily browsed. For a COLLECTIVE WORK, such as a sound recording of folk tales or a book of plays, listing the individual titles may be important. Any unusual details of binding, title, or edition that may confuse the patron may be recorded in this area.

The notes area begins a new paragraph. List each in the same order as the descriptive elements: notes about the title first, those about the series last. Notes can be added to any

Notes Area

level of description, but are never obligatory and should be added judiciously. Some libraries may find it simpler to catalog at Level One, and supply descriptive details (such as a subtitle) in the notes as needed. Notes provide useful information, but also add to the expense of producing the record.

Standard Numbers and Terms of Availability

International Standard Book Numbers and the International Standard Series Numbers (ISBN and ISSN) are numbers uniquely assigned to almost every book and series published. Some books have both an ISBN and an ISSN. These numbers are often noted in publishers' catalogs and advertisements and used in ordering. Place the ISSN with the series parentheses and the ISBN above the tracings. Use any standard numbers found on the materials when cataloging, even for First Level Description. No special punctuation is required.

Terms of Availability, the price of the item, is not recommended for inclusion in the public catalog. Many libraries do, however, record the cost of items in the shelf list in order to assess fines for damaged or lost materials.

Entries for most library materials can be made by using these general rules. Cartographic items, serials, and complex multimedia sets are considered later.

SUMMARY

Descriptive cataloging insures that the catalog identifies and describes each item in the collection. Without catalog descriptions, users would be forced to examine the items themselves in order to use the collection. The requirements for details of description vary from library to library because researchers, gothic romance enthusiasts, elementary school students, and business people have different information needs.

Collections that house all formats and have a single catalog should supply details that are not essential for a one-format catalog. The cataloger who must type each card will describe items less fully than one who can purchase prepared copy. Whereas AACR2 provides guidelines for describing all formats, the cataloger must decide on the level of description and the use of other options, such as the GMD.

In other areas there is little room for individual choice. Because libraries may wish to share resources, the cataloger should, by relying on the correct Source of Information, record the required elements with standard terminology and ab-

ELEMENTS OF DESCRIPTION	MAJOR POINTS TO CONSIDER WHEN LAYING OUT THE DESCRIPTION
Title	Transcribe exactly as it appears Lengthy titles may be shortened Capitalize only proper names Include apostrophes and commas as given Construct a missing title and enclose it in brackets
GMD	Use this option according to local guidelines Select from the appropriate GMD list, terms should not vary
Parallel Titles and Sub-titles	Level One — Omit Level Two — Transcribe exactly as given, using rules for title proper
Statements of Responsibility	Name only those prominently featured on the item Level One — Name only those first listed for any responsible function Level Two — Include all functions and those prominently named as responsible
Edition	Include in all levels Level Two — Include any statement of responsibility given Use arabic numerals and standard abbreviations
Publication Details	Level One — List first given publisher, producer, distributor, etc. and date Level Two — Add place to all publishers, producers, distributors, etc. as given Use the most recent date given Supply an approximate date for undated items; enclose in square brackets
Physical Details	Record the physical properties of the item, using standard materials designations. Terms should not vary Use arabic numerals and standard abbreviations Level One — Include only extent of item Level Two — Include additional physical details, such as dimensions, time, speed, size of film, etc.
Series	Level One — Omit Level Two — Transcribe series title as it appears, using rules for title proper Include statement of responsibility and ISSN when given
Notes	Create as appropriate
Standard Number	Include in all levels when available

Figure 4-7

breviations, with ISBD punctuation, and in proper order. In this way the catalog will be capable of fulfilling not only today's information needs, but also those of the future.

CHAPTER REVIEW

Terms to understand:

alternative title	parallel title
cataloging in publication (CIP)	specific materials
collective title	designations
collective work	supplied title
general materials designations	technical reading
ISBN	title proper
other title information	verso

Descriptive cataloging:

Eight elements of description.
Punctuated with machine-readable punctuation (ISBD).
Chosen from the sources of information.
Described with one of three levels of description using standard
    terminology.

The process of constructing an entry:

Before identifying and recording the descriptive elements, determine format, source of information, and level of description by technical reading.

CHAPTER 5

PROVIDING ACCESS POINTS: AACR2, PART II

A RECORD must have headings if it is ever to be found in the catalog. The cataloger assigns these access points after completing the description. When standardized they gather together items with common bibliographic features, allowing the catalog to show how many works by Jane Austen, or which editions of *Hamlet*, are available. This permits the second purpose of the catalog, that of organizing the collection bibliographically, to be achieved. Part II of AACR2 is the basic tool for choosing and recording headings.

MAIN ENTRY

Recently librarians have been questioning the validity of the concept of main entry. When cataloging information is retrieved by a computer, main and added entry are meaningless terms, because information can be retrieved from any one of several access points. Indeed, with the unit card system, in which the cataloger adds access points to cards that otherwise look alike, both main and added entries contain complete information. Nonetheless, it is useful to have one standard access point, universally agreed upon, which will always lead to an individual item. Because this entry makes it easier to communicate and to share materials with other libraries the rules in AACR2 are carefully followed in order to standardize the main entry.

In reality, catalogers have few choices, because main and added entries are nearly always selected from bibliographic details found in the Chief Source of Information. In most cases main entry is an author or creator; the title; or a corporate body, the agency responsible for the work's publication or distribution. Authors have always been first choice for main entry (at least in the Western world) and when there is a person obviously responsible for the work, that name is chosen. If more than one person is involved, the principal author or the first name listed is selected.

When the term author was defined during the 19th century for the purposes of cataloging, the definition was expanded to include not only editors and compilers, but corporate bodies as well. This interpretation led to a number of complex problems in this century as corporations and government agencies multiplied, divided, changed names and extended their activities. As a result the average library user today has little chance of locating anything under a corporate name. AACR2 restricts the circumstances for entering corporations as main entries, and denies main entry to editors and compilers. Under this code, main entry as the name of a corporate body can occur only when the item is definitely a statement about its internal operations and activities.

Title main entry is assigned when a work has four or more authors; when the author is unknown or cannot be determined; when only an editor or compiler is named; when the work is issued by a corporate body but does not fit a category for corporate entry, or is regarded as sacred scripture.

Access points can also be assigned to any other names such as joint authors, editors, compilers, and the like. These added entries provide additional access points.

These simple guidelines will solve most problems of choosing main entries, but some problems will remain, because corporate structure is difficult to understand, and sacred scripture follows special rules.

After entries have been selected, the name or title is recorded. Even when this is taken from the Chief Source of Information, however, questions about form may persist. For instance names may be in an unfamiliar language, works may be issued by joint committees, and papers presented by heads of state. AACR2 provides guidance for recording access points consistently.

PERSONAL NAMES
AS ENTRIES
　　Author as
　　Main Entry

A personal author is an individual chiefly responsible for the content of a work. Operas, plays, maps, sonatas, novels, and paintings can all be works of personal authorship and are cataloged under single, principal, or first-named authors who are easily identified from the Chief Source of Information. When a work has been created by two or more people, the first, or principal, person named in the Chief Source is the main entry and the others are added entries.

It is not so simple to identify the principal author of a work of MIXED RESPONSIBILITY, such as revisions, adaptations, or books containing text and illustrations by different people. What is the correct procedure for cataloging a journalist's interview with a member of the government, or a recording of a performer's adaptation of a composer's score?

Such works fall into two broadly defined categories: modifications of previously published materials, and collaborations producing new works. A modification of a work is usually entered under the new author if there have been substantial changes in the content of the work or its medium. If the modification is merely an updating, rearrangement, or abridgement, enter under the original author. The deciding factor is the amount of the original work that remains. When *Hamlet* is transferred verbatim to a sound recording it is still *Hamlet* and is entered under Shakespeare. *Hamlet* as retold for children by Charles and Mary Lamb is entered under Lamb. The musical *My Fair Lady* retains some of the language of George Bernard Shaw's play *Pygmalion,* but for the most part was written and composed by Alan Jay Lerner and Frederick Loewe, who get the credit in the catalog. The cataloger is not obliged to read editions, or compare films with texts to determine content change. Accept whatever is listed in the Chief Source of Information, preferring the original author's name when that has been retained. Children's librarians who prefer to have all adaptations, revisions, and simplified versions under the original author can achieve this by providing an added entry for that person.

Another kind of decision is made when an item cannot be regarded as the work of a single person. Examples include children's picture books with both authors and illustrators; autobiographies written in collaboration with professional writers; and the letters of famous people selected and edited by others. In these cases the cataloger must decide whether the work is a collaboration, and if so, enter it as an item with joint authors. In this case the main entry will be the principal, or first-named author, and the statement of responsibility will follow the Chief Source of Information. If, on the basis of the Chief Source, the cataloger judges it the work of one author and not a collaboration, it should be entered as such.

After the cataloger has selected a personal name as a main (or added) entry that name is normally recorded in the form given in the Chief Source. Care should be taken, however, to insure that works created by the same person are found together in the catalog. The cataloger is responsible for the record of an entire collection, and items in that collection should be gathered bibliographically. Unfortunately, personal names are not recorded uniformly in Chief Sources of Information. Sometimes a full name will appear, sometimes initials, or even nicknames. The rules call for entry under "the most frequently used name," whether it is a nickname, pseudonym,

Recording Personal Names

title of nobility, initials, or other appellation. This does not mean that the cataloger must do extensive research. When a personal name appears in the CIP data, accept it; otherwise record it as it appears in the Chief Source of Information. If the author's name appears in several forms the cataloger makes a decision, consulting reference sources if necessary.

Sometimes main entry differs from the statement of responsibility in the descriptive paragraph. Samuel Clemens wrote under the pseudonym Mark Twain. If the work is entered under his pseudonym, but gives his real name on the title page, the statement of responsibility differs as in the following example.

> Twain, Mark.
> A Connecticut yankee in King Arthur's Court / by Samuel Langhorne Clemens.

This procedure also applies to authors who use only their initials or nicknames.

Also accept the Chief Source of Information for those people who publish under pseudonyms, or change their names.

> Findlay, John Niemeyer.
> Kant and the transcendental object : a hermeneutic study / by J. N. Findlay.

It is not necessary to add dates of birth and death or biographical information. Only when several people with the same name appear in the catalog is it a good idea to distinguish between them by adding information.

> Burrell, Robert Michael.
> Iran, Afghanistan, Pakistan: Tension and dilemmas / R. M. Burrell and Alvin J. Cottrell.
> (Joint authors. Name on title page, R. M. Burrell, but other works already entered under Robert Michael Burrell.)

> Carroll, Lewis (Not Charles Dodgson).
> (Lewis Carroll is the commonly recognized pseudonym of the author of *Alice in Wonderland*.)

> Buchwald, Art.
> "I am not a crook" / Art Buchwald.
> (Commonly used nickname.)

> Rossetti, Anton, 1746-1792.
> Rossetti, Dante Gabriel, 1828-1882.
> (Dates are used to distinguish between the two.)

H. D. (Hilda Doolittle)
Lawrence, D. H. (David Herbert)
(Full name in parentheses added for identification.)

Even when relying on the Chief Source of Information, the cataloger may still have doubts. Forenames should be used for royalty, saints, and members of religious orders, and clarified by a designation, or identifying phrase.

Charles II, King of Great Britain
John XXIII, Pope
Beatrix, Queen of the Netherlands
Edward, Brother
Benedict, Saint

For compound names, or names with prefixes, follow the form of the language in which the author writes. Hyphenated names are treated as a single word.

DuMaurier, Daphne
de la Mare, Walter
Day-Lewis, Cecil
Lloyd George, David
Goethe, Johann Wolfgang von

Classical writers are entered under the names by which they are best known in English, e.g., Horace, Cicero, Virgil.

Titles of nobility are used if the person is commonly known by that title and appears under it in reference sources.

Mountbatten of Burma, Louis Mountbatten, 1st Earl.

Few problems will arise if the name is recorded in the form generally used by the author, or in the form given in the Chief Source of Information. There will always be someone, however, who searches for Stendhal under Beyle, Unamuno y Jugo under Jugo, or Van Greenaway under Greenaway, and CROSS REFERENCES should therefore be made from the name not used to the other, e.g.,

Clemens, Samuel Langhorne
        see
Twain, Mark

la Mare, Walter de
        see
de la Mare, Walter

Corporate Bodies as Entries

A corporate body is an organization or group that acts as a single entity and is identified by a collective name. Examples include associations, institutions, businesses, government agencies, religious bodies, churches, and conferences. The publications of corporate bodies are very numerous and cataloging them can be a challenge. AACR2 limits the occasions on which corporations appear as main entries.

The code enumerates those items that can be considered candidates for corporate entry:

1. Items of an administrative nature such as newsletters, annual reports, regulations, rules, and membership lists.

2. Legal documents such as laws, treaties, decrees, and court decisions.

3. Collective thought of a body such as a statement issued by the American Medical Association, or a committee report from the Parent-Teacher Association.

4. Works that record the activities of a conference, such as the White House Conference on Aging, or an academic symposium.

5. Works that are the products of established performing groups such as The Who, the Amadeus String Quartet, and the New York Philharmonic, when their responsibility goes beyond mere performance.

If a work does not fit any of these categories, do not enter it under a corporate name even if the corporation paid for the publication and printed its name on it. Whereas corporate publications are found in every collection, cataloging copy for them is rarely available. The public library can be expected to have directories of local agencies, manuals from local governments, and annual business reports; school libraries have college catalogs and illustrated catalogs from art galleries; college libraries house materials produced by conferences and symposiums; and church libraries collect reports from missions and records of conferences. Such materials often constitute the bulk of special library collections. Although some of these materials may be left uncataloged, others should be added to the general collection, and the rules should therefore be understood.

Recording Corporate Names

The basic rule for corporate bodies is the same as that for personal authors. Enter under the name most likely to be known by the user. Entry under corporate body is more confusing than entry under person, because these bodies change their names frequently, names are hard to track down, and corporations often contain many subordinate agencies.

Under the present rules, when a corporate body changes names it becomes a new entity and normally the cataloger does not worry about tying the names together. When a corporate body lists its name differently in the Chief Source of Information and in its various publications, select the name appearing in a more formal position (head of the title, statement of responsibility, etc.). If that doesn't work, decide which name is most common and choose its briefest form.

ERIC — not Educational Resources Information Center
NATO — not North Atlantic Treaty Organization

More and more information is being presented in the form of reports from conferences, workshops, symposiums. These are defined by AACR2 as meetings convened, "for the purpose of discussing and acting on topics of common interest." When the title of such a meeting appears in the Chief Source of Information, that name may be used as the main entry. Add the number of the conference, and the date and place in parentheses when known.

Windsor Conference on Comparative Urban Economics and Development (1972: Univ. of Windsor)

Canadian Mathematical Congress (1973: Univ. of Western Ontario)

IFAS Symposium on Identification and System Parameter Estimation (1973: The Hague)

Conference on Computers in the Undergraduate Curriculum (2nd: Dartmouth College: 1971)

Entry under a corporate body presents one problem that entering under author does not: people do not have subdivisions, or subordinate and related bodies. The general rule in these situations is to enter directly under the subordinate name when it is distinctive and used on publications. For example:

Air Pollution Technical Information Center

This center, a subordinate body, is part of the Environmental Protection Agency. It is entered in the catalog as an independent unit since it does not depend on its parent body for identification. In the following cases the sub-heading must be under the name of a higher body:

1. The subordinate body's name includes a word such as

"department" or "division," indicating a relationship with a higher body:

Organization for Economic Cooperation and Development. Economic Prospects Division.

2. A committee's name implies subordination.

American Institute of Certified Public Accountants. Committee on Stockbrokerage Auditing.

3. Subordinate or related bodies whose names are so general that the name of a higher body is needed for identification.

Republican Party. National Committee.

4. Institutes or departments within universities and colleges:

Pratt Insitute. School of Architecture.

5. Enter as a subordinate a name that is included in the entire name of a larger institution such as the University of Georgia Library.

University of Georgia. Library.

The situation becomes more complicated when the unit issuing the work is the lowest link of an organization's hierarchy. If the entire hierarchy is listed it will be extremely long. Omit any part of the chain not needed to link the smaller body with the larger one. For example, United Nations Department of International Economic and Social Affairs, Center for Social Development and Humanitarian Affairs is entered as:

United Nations. Center for Social Development and Humanitarian Affairs.

Because there is only one such center in the U.N. it will not lose its identity when entered directly under United Nations.

As anyone who has searched through the United States entries of a catalog realizes, rules for corporate bodies also include agencies of the government. Partly because these entries were becoming so cumbersome, the principles of entry under government bodies were simplified by AACR2, and are now identical to those for non-government bodies. If the agency has a unique name that does not suggest dependent status, it is entered under its own name.

> National Science Foundation
> Library of Congress
> National Library of Medicine

However, if the name of the subordinate unit implies that it is dependent, or if the name of the government is required to identify the agency, enter it as a subordinate body.

> United States. Commission on Civil Rights.
> Georgia. Judicial Planning Committee.
> New Hampshire. Office of State Planning.

Not only states, towns, and countries are entered as corporate bodies, but also the official acts of the heads of these entities. The form is as follows: government, title with years of incumbency, brief form of person's name:

> United States. President (1961-1963; Kennedy)
> United Kingdom. Sovereign (1952-   ; Elizabeth II)

This form is only for official publications. Material that does not fall into this category is entered in the same way as a personal author:

> Kennedy, John Fitzgerald
>   Profiles in courage

It is often necessary for the cataloger to distinguish between corporate names or government bodies by adding geographic location. For instance, a First National Bank might exist in any hamlet and there is a Court of Appeals in every state. The general rule is to use the English form of the name as found in a gazetteer. When there is a need to distinguish between places with the same name, add the name of the next largest geographical unit.

Geographic Names

> First National Bank (Springfield, Mo.)
> First National Bank (Springfield, Ill.)

The title is such an important means of identifying an item that when this cannot be found it is invented by the cataloger, which is not true of other areas of description. Some cata-

Titles as Entries

logers argue that title makes a better choice than author for main entry, because there is only one title, whereas author main entry often presents a number of candidates. Non-book materials, for example, are simpler to enter under title, because when there are several people involved in the performance of a piece of music, or the creation of a film, a principal author cannot easily be selected. Corporate entry is not always a convenient access point. AACR2 defines the concept of author very narrowly. Editors and compilers are not considered authors; corporate bodies can only be authors under restricted rules. In these cases, when the author is unknown, or when there are more than three authors, enter under title. Sacred scripture has long been entered under title.

Recording
Titles

Simple title entry is not a problem. During the descriptive process the title is identified and recorded from the Chief Source of Information. When title is selected as an entry, it is already constructed. But the second purpose of the catalog has still to be met.

Uniform
Titles

The cataloger is responsible for bringing together different editions of the same work. These often have different individual titles, such as *Alice in Wonderland,* and *Alice's Adventures in Wonderland.* When the same work has different titles in different editions, the cataloger selects a uniform title that brings them together in the catalog.

Catalogers have long had rules for using uniform titles for certain categories of works: sacred scripture (the Bible or Koran), laws and treaties, and anonymous classics (*Mother Goose, Beowulf,* and the *Arabian Nights*). The need for uniform titles has also been recognized when title is used for an added entry. *Hamlet,* for example, may have different titles in its various editions, but users will expect to find *Hamlet* under either Shakespeare or *Hamlet,* so a UNIFORM TITLE is used as the title access point. This is also called the FILING TITLE in some cataloging manuals.

Because sacred scripture exists in numerous editions, they are entered in the catalog under uniform titles. To the uniform title add language, version, and year:

Bible. English. Douay. 1910.
Talmud. English.
Koran. English.

Selections are arranged thus:

Bible. O.T. Ruth. English. 1970.

Anonymous classics are works that have been available since before 1500, have appeared under a variety of titles, and whose authors are unknown. In these cases uniform titles are used for the main entry regardless of variant editions.

Mother Goose.
Brian Wildsmith's Mother Goose.

When a uniform title is used as main entry the hanging indention card format is not used. The card follows the format used for author main entry instead.

Beowulf.
The Therkelin transcripts of Beowulf / translated by Kemp Malone.

Like other adaptations, however, anonymous classics are entered under the name of the adaptor when the text has been rewritten.

Hosford, Dorothy.
By his own might: the battles of Beowulf / Dorothy Hosford; drawings by Lasylo Matulay.

Williams, Jay.
The horn of Roland / Jay Williams; illus. by Sean Merriseris.

No standard uniform titles have been created for works published since 1500, so when a work has appeared under varying titles the cataloger should select the best known. Use the following forms:

Shakespeare, William.
[Hamlet]
The tragedy of Hamlet, the Prince of Denmark / by William Shakespeare.

Musical works often have popular titles in addition to those given by their composers. Using music reference tools, the cataloger creates uniform titles to bring the works together.

Other situations also call for decisions about uniform titles. An abridgement may be published under a different title from the original edition; a book or film first released in England may bear a different title when issued in America; different editions of the same reference work or textbook series may have different titles. Uniform titles should be created according to the cataloger's expectation of users' needs.

ADDED ENTRIES

After recording the main entry, the problem of selecting and recording added entries remains. The main reason to select additional access points is the judgment that someone may look for that item under that heading. Most libraries choose to make added entries according to their staffing resources and the needs of their users. Added entries can usually be found in the Chief Source of Information, but an added entry does not have to be made for every bibliographic detail listed there.

Added entries are normally made in the same form as main entries, but titles are sometimes traced differently. Occasionally there may be a need for access to a partial title, alternative title, or subtitle, and an additional title tracing will be provided. For example, the Golden Press published a great many titles for juveniles that start with "The Golden Book of": *The Golden Book of Facts and Figures, The Golden Book of Fun and Nonsense, The Golden Book of the Civil War, The Golden Book of the Renaissance.* Users may be inclined to search under Facts and Figures, especially if this phrase is printed in larger letters. It makes sense therefore to provide additional title access in the tracings:

I. Title II. Title: Facts and figures

CROSS REFERENCES

Because the cataloger can never be certain that users will seek information under the main and added entries that have been selected, *see* and *see also* references are used. *See* guides the user from a name or term that is not employed, or employed in a different form, to the relevant entry. The card for "Leonardo," for example, may read: "See da Vinci, Leonardo." *See also* guides the user from a name or term that is employed to another, related entry that will provide additional information. If a catalog conflict is created by following different codes, an author's works are entered under two names (Twain, Mark and Clemens, Samuel Langhorne). Then *see also* references guide the user from one to the other.

Unfortunately, in many libraries that have been buying copy for their catalogs, the cross reference structure seems to have fallen into disuse. It is far too easy to purchase catalog cards, file them away, and ignore other aspects of catalog maintenance that make it a better tool for users. If department store catalogs and telephone books find it necessary to use these references, certainly the more complex library or media center catalog should offer such aids. The use of cross references is a matter of judgment on the part of catalogers.

AUTHORITY FILES

Many decisions are involved in the process of selecting and recording entries. To insure consistency some libraries maintain AUTHORITY FILES to record these decisions. Most authority files are on cards that give the chosen form of entry with any cross references that have been used. When physically convenient, a library's catalog is the best authority for forms of headings, however, it does not record cross references. A separate record for cross references allows all traces of a name or title to be removed from the catalog when a work is withdrawn. Usually authority files are placed near the shelf list.

SUMMARY

Entries, also called access points, provide a way of entry to the information stored in the catalog. Standardization of these access points is important if works are to be related and gathered together in the catalog according to their bibliographic features. If libraries are to share materials and information through networks, they must agree on standard ways to identify works.

Catalogers select a main entry for each work. When an author, or authors, are clearly responsible for the work, main entry is under the personal name. Under certain clearly defined circumstances works are entered under corporate names (which includes government bodies). Other works, including those with compilers and editors, are entered under title.

If all the works of an author, and all editions and titles of a work, are to be located in the catalog, the forms of the entries must be standardized. Usually the form as found in the Chief Source of Information is adequate; when there is conflict, select the form in most common use. Classics and sacred scriptures frequently have many variant titles which are standardized by a uniform title.

Even when cataloging information is purchased, it is necessary to do original cataloging with corporate publications, as many of these may be of limited or local issue. By following the code these materials can be integrated with the catalog and the rest of the collection.

See and *see also* references are important as they guide users to correct, or to additional headings.

CHAPTER REVIEW

Terms to understand:

author entry	mixed responsibility
conflict	*see also* reference
corporate entry	*see* reference
cross references	title entry
filing title	uniform title

Catalog headings or access points:

Based on bibliographic details
Recorded according to AACR2.
Include author, title, and corporate entries.

Author entries:

May be under a personal author.
The only, principal, or first-named author in the Chief Source
of Information.
When responsibility is mixed, either an adaptation or a
collaboration.
Follow authority of Chief Source.

Corporate entries:

Under circumstances defined by AACR2, works can be entered under corporate name as found in the Chief Source of
Information. Use brief forms, entering directly under the
name of a subordinate body of an organization when that
smaller body has a distinct identity. Otherwise under largest
body where it does not lose identity. If needed, identify by
place.

Title entry:

Use a uniform title form for sacred scripture, anonymous
classics, musical works, and variant titles. Record the entries
as found in Chief Source of Information unless this causes
conflict in catalog. In such cases, use the most common term.
Tie decisions together with cross references.
Record the decision in authority file.

CHAPTER 6

ORGANIZING BY SUBJECT

USERS are often seeking not specific items that can be retrieved by an author or title heading, but materials dealing with particular subjects. Identification of the library's holdings by subject is therefore one of the catalog's most important functions. There is evidence that King Assurbanipal's librarians practiced a form of classification by shelving arrangement, and during the European Middle Ages libraries were commonly arranged in this way rather than by author or title.

In order to identify library materials as individual items, or as part of a group, catalogers describe each work and provide standard access points. These are also the objectives of subject cataloging: to identify individual works whose subject is known, and to gather works on the same subject together. Although librarians have taken different approaches to the organization of knowledge, they have all struggled with the basic problem of how to relate materials to each other on the shelf, while relating them intellectually in the catalog.

FIXED VERSUS RELATIVE LOCATION

One of the oldest methods of gathering subjects on the shelf and in the catalog is FIXED LOCATION. In this arrangement all pamphlets are placed in chest A, and all books are stacked in chest B. Or all musical works are in the North Room and all art items in the South Room. They can be arranged by size, by order received, or in any other way that appeals to the cataloger. Today, collections on CLOSED SHELVES, which prohibit public access, are often shelved in fixed locations, usually to save space. In collections that cannot be browsed, such as a film library, fixed location is also a reasonable option. Library collections tend to grow, however, and someday the pamphlets will not fit into chest A, and a wing must be added to the South Room for the art works. Are there to be two art collections now, and then three and four? Or is a new scheme to be developed and the whole collection rearranged?

As a partial solution to the problem of growth, fixed collections can be arranged by accession number (order of purchase) which does allow new acquisitions to be added at one end. Film libraries often follow this scheme. Films are placed in strict numerical order by purchase, and a catalog provides access. Since film users will rarely wish to browse in a row of cans, film librarians don't need to provide physical access to subjects. Otherwise, they would have to abandon fixed location.

The majority of libraries in the United States have an OPEN SHELF arrangement in which users browse. Most library materials are packaged to attract attention and many patrons, once they have found the correct subject area, prefer to select materials personally. In an open shelf library users find call numbers in the catalog that guide them to shelf locations. Call numbers indicate subjects, and materials with related subjects and adjacent call numbers are shelved together. This can only be achieved by a RELATIVE LOCATION system in which items are not fixed to any one position in the library, but can be moved to and fro as required so that new items can be intershelved with others dealing with the same subject. The design of a relative location system remained an unsolved problem for centuries.

CLASSIFICATION

Classification is the putting together of like things, and to catalogers this means the grouping of library materials into subject areas. First, however, there must be agreement on the subjects themselves. Because material in a library can, in theory, represent all the world's store of information, most classification schemes have started with a philosophical division of human knowledge. The most influential scheme was that of Francis Bacon, who in the 17th century divided knowledge into three general categories: history, poetry, and philosophy. Thomas Jefferson, who owned 7,000 volumes, cataloged them according to Bacon's divisions. The Library of Congress acquired this collection in 1815 and retained the classification system until the end of the 19th century.

MELVIL DEWEY

In 1873 Melvil Dewey was an undergraduate working in the library of Amherst College, which was arranged at that time in a cumbersome fixed location. Dewey was interested in developing a system that would allow for relative location. At that time there was no model he could imitate, for no large library was completely classified. A number of librarians had experimented with schemes based on Bacon's outline, but no one had devised a simple expandable system. Then, "One Sunday during a long sermon by Pres. Stearns, while I lookt stedfastly at him without hearing a word, my mind absorbed in the vital problem, the solution flasht over me so that I jumpt in my seat and came near shouting *Eureka*." The solution that came to Dewey was the idea of using numbers with decimal points as subject notations. Thus Dewey created a relative location system with a universal notation that is easy to understand and can be expanded almost indefinitely by adding numbers after the decimal.

During its evolution through 19 editions, and its growth from 48 pages to three volumes, Dewey's classification system has gathered critics. His subject divisions have been found archaic, his thinking ethnocentric, and his outline of knowledge unoriginal. These complaints are beside the point, however, because the system is practical, provides for relative location, furnishes a call number for shelf location, and brings together like works. More libraries use Dewey than any other classification system and it is unlikely that this will change.

Dewey closely supervised each edition and stipulated that a foundation would continue to do so after his death. Today Forest Press, a division of the foundation, works closely with Library of Congress, and LC cards indicate a DDC notation. The system is now revised every seven years.

Meanwhile, the old Jeffersonian scheme was still in use at the Library of Congress, but when, in 1897, the one and a half million volumes were moved to new quarters, the Library began to assess the merits of the Dewey system, and that of Charles Cutter, whose system can be expanded by using a combination of both letters and numbers. Dewey refused to allow LC to modify his system in any way. Cutter agreed to modification, but died shortly after. LC ultimately used a system of letters and numbers derived from Cutter. Like the DDC, LCC is based on a classification by discipline, but in this case, not so much the entire world of knowledge, but the world of knowledge as represented by the collection in the Library of Congress. As the collection has grown, LCC has expanded, but revisions depend on the needs of the library, not on the expansion of knowledge in general.

LCC is composed of letters and numbers, and uses 26 letters of the alphabet for its main classes. Unlike DDC, which has one schedule and is the invention of one man, LCC has a group of schedules, each produced by a different

LIBRARY
OF CONGRESS

67

team. LCC achieves its relative location by using the letters of the alphabet, and allows for 26 main classes. Each class can be subdivided by use of a second alphabet AA-AZ. Each subclass can then be divided arithmetically, 1-9999. More letters and numbers can be added as required.

TK Class number for technology	RG Medicine
9153 A subdivision number	525 Subdivision
G76 "Author number"	F37 "Author number"

Library of Congress cards are printed with LCC numbers, which are used in many academic libraries. Because revisions are continuous, there are a number of schedules — new, revised, and reprinted with changes.

UNIVERSAL
DECIMAL
CLASSIFICATION

The UDC is not an original scheme, but a derivative of DDC. The UDC, developed in Europe at the end of the 19th century, is a practical classification based, not on theory, but on the problems of retrieving information from pamphlets, reports, and periodicals. It is basically a system for coding information numerically so that an item, once coded and filed, can be readily found from any access point.

The basic notation of UDC is single arabic numbers, rather than the minimum three of DDC. Thus religions are 2 rather than 200. A period is placed after every three digits. UDC also has auxiliary symbols that indicate some facet of information: time, space, language, documents with two subjects, points of view, relationships, and so on. UDC is an international code and can be used to specify almost any subject.

UDC has been a great success in special libraries and information centers. In libraries, where not shelf arrangement but indexing is the major consideration, UDC has proved useful. Journals, indexes, and abstracting services, especially in the field of engineering, have also adopted it. It is now obligatory in Russian scientific and technical libraries. It can be used alone, or with other systems, and computer applications are being studied. UDC has both the faults and the strengths of the system from which it derived.

READER
INTEREST
CLASSIFICATION

RIC was developed by Detroit Public Library to serve those collections whose users prefer to select materials by browsing. Materials are placed in large groups centered around topics such as "current affairs," "your family," and "the consumer." These groups can be managed in several ways. One alternative is to use the group term in place of the call number on the book and in the catalog cards. This means the arrangement will be permanent. Another way is to pencil in temporary markings that can be erased when the material is returned to the general collection.

RIC has been used in bookmobiles, small branch libraries, and collections for children and young adults. Little information has been collected on its usefulness, but many librarians have reported positive results. However, almost all libraries cater to topical interests by means of exhibits or temporary groupings, and this seems more practical than committing a collection to permanent RIC classification.

Other classification schemes exist, most of them the work of individuals who attempted to create a perfect system. Even if a perfect classification scheme were devised, however, it is doubtful whether any library would adopt it. Because DDC and LCC numbers are so readily available in the form of MARC, CIP, and purchased cards, libraries are able to save time that would otherwise be spent on classification. Furthermore, few libraries are willing to spend money on reclassification. During the 1960s, a number of libraries changed from DDC to LCC but as economic conditions have worsened, that trend has slowed. Indeed, many librarians question the cost of any reclassification, even when this is done to adapt to a new revision of a schedule.

SUBJECT HEADINGS

Classification schemes make it possible to shelve similar subjects together, but this alone does not solve all problems of subject access. Users must be able to find which notations have been assigned to a given subject; they must have access to materials that cover more than one topic; and they should be aware of what a library has on a given subject.

The problems of subject catalogs have also been studied for many years. Headings derived from titles and from catchwords, and broad headings with subdivisions have been tried. The theory of SPECIFIC SUBJECT ENTRY was not defined until Cutter had described the two principal objectives of the catalog—to identify works individually and as part of a group. Subject heading theory requires that a work be assigned as specific a subject heading as can be identified. So that the user will be aware of all other material the library has on the subject, headings are not made up by the librarian, but chosen from a standard list.

Subject control is easier to achieve in theory than in reality, because neither the cataloger nor the user can be sure how either is going to interpret a subject, or what words either will choose for access. Catalogers can reduce confusion by using standard lists and by creating a network of *see* and *see also* references, but choosing a subject heading is often challenging.

TYPES OF
SUBJECT
HEADINGS

The simplest subject heading is a noun. The user searching for information on tigers will probably look for the heading TIGERS. This type of subject heading usually causes few problems, but the singular and the plural of a noun may have different meanings, for example; drama and dramas, theater and theaters. Bridge can be a game or a structure. There is also the problem of those who will look for tigers under ANIMALS or even MAMMALS.

Some noun headings are expanded with adjectives in order to make them more specific. But this creates another problem: will users look under the adjective or the noun? Because opinions have differed, we find both AMERICAN LITERATURE and PHILOSOPHY, CHINESE.

Some subjects are so closely related that compound headings are necessary, for example, TECHNOLOGY AND CIVILIZATION, CITIES AND TOWNS, CLOCKS AND WATCHES. Even if this concept is correct, there remains the problem of which word should be first.

Other concepts require a phrase in order to be specific: ACTING FOR TELEVISION, SOCIAL PROBLEMS IN LITERATURE, DRAMA IN EDUCATION. Subject headings can also be made more specific by adding place, literary form, or period, a process referred to as subdivision.

During the last decade attempts have been made to program computers to create subject headings. In order to do this successfully the computer needs full access to texts, and it is unlikely that all library materials will be in machine-readable form for many years. Key word approaches have been tried, but shades of meaning cannot be recognized by computers. For the foreseeable future, human catalogers will be responsible for the subject headings assigned to most library materials. This process can be computer assisted, however, with the computer assuming responsibility for generating references.

PRECIS (PRESERVED
CONTEXT INDEX
SYSTEM)

PRECIS is a computer-assisted system developed by the British National Bibliography during the 1960s and used to index a variety of bibliographies and catalogs for both print and non-print formats, especially in British Commonwealth countries. In PRECIS, a subject heading is replaced by a "string"; a series of terms summarizing the content of a work. Each term in the string is related to the terms immediately preceding and following it. Terms are recorded starting with the widest context and moving to the most specific. For example, a string for a work dealing with evaluation of management in industry in Japan presents the subject in summary form as follows:

Japan — industry — management — evaluation

Any or every term in the string can serve as the entry term for the user. The terms are kept in logical order so the links between them are not broken. A two-line entry structure is employed.

The lead is the term that functions as the entry point for the user. The qualifiers place the lead in successively wider contexts. The display is a term of narrower reference.

> MANAGEMENT. — Industry. — Japan.
>   Evaluation
>
> INDUSTRY. — Japan.
>   Management. Evaluation.

The indexers put only a single string into the computer, which contains instructions on how the terms should be manipulated into entries; the address to which the entries refer; and all the *see* and *see also* references (called RINS, or Reference Indicator Numbers) appropriate to the terms in the string.

Once the record has entered the computer, the human task is completed and the machine takes over. Not only does it generate all indicated entries and references, but it also sorts and generates a magnetic tape which can be used to create catalogs and other bibliographic products.

SUBJECT HEADING LISTS

Most catalogers still assign subject headings not with the assistance of technology, but by using a standard subject heading list and hoping that by following its directives, they will be able to guide most library users successfully.

The most commonly used subject heading lists are *Library of Congress Subject Headings* (LCSH) and the *Sears List of Subject Headings*. LCSH, first published in 1909 and now in its ninth edition, is a list of subject headings used in the Library of Congress. These subject headings are also printed on LC cards, on MARC tapes, and in the Cataloging in Publication data found on the verso of the title page of a book. General directions for using the list are printed in the introduction. *Sears,* first published in 1923, is intended for small general collections.

Special libraries, which deal with particular subject areas in depth, need more specific terms than those provided by either of these general lists. Medical libraries, for example, use MeSH (Medical Subject Headings) and other fields have similar lists. MeSH was developed by the National Library of Medicine as part of its computer retrieval system and is not so much a subject heading list as a THESAURUS. Computer subject retrieval requires a strictly controlled list, because the machine will only accept terms that are listed. As more and more subject searches are being done with the aid of the computer, other data bases have developed thesauri for strictly limited subject areas such as the ERIC (Educational Resources Information Center) thesaurus. Even when no computer is involved, many groups publish specialized lists to be used in conjunction with a general list, and religious denominations often publish and update such lists regularly in their journals.

Special lists are developed for special interests, but general lists attempt to provide subject access for library users in general, and must therefore sacrifice precision and topicality. LCSH and Sears are revised periodically, but unless the catalog is an on-line computer, revision is an expensive and time-consuming chore not to be undertaken lightly. Long after travelers were flying in jets, LCSH was guiding them to information under the heading "aeroplane."

When, during the late 1960s, minority groups and women began to assert that social prejudice is reflected in language, subject heading lists were accused of bias. Librarians have long been aware that the Dewey classification scheme is biased and revisions have been made to overcome this problem. Yet it is difficult to imagine a user becoming incensed over a call number no matter what bias it might express to the librarian. Such headings in the public catalog as NEGROES—SOCIAL AND MORAL CONDITION, DELINQUENT WOMEN, and JEWS AS DOCTORS are a different matter. These and other headings have now been revised, and Sears has developed an alternate list for Blacks. Users are entitled to subject headings that are not only useful but also appear impartial, and catalogers should attempt to make subject headings reflect current social conditions.

SUMMARY

Department stores, supermarkets, and libraries all try to classify their contents so the patrons can find and compare the items they want. Whereas department stores must categorize apparel, librarians have an even more difficult task. A library contains a large part of the accumulated wisdom of the world, and the preoccupations of users are not as easily measured as their clothing sizes. By using a notation system, classification provides call numbers that locate each item according to subject. The two most popular systems in the United States are the Dewey Decimal, which uses numbers and decimals, and the Library of Congress, which combines letters and numbers. The user can locate these call numbers by searching for subject headings or descriptors in a catalog. To provide for standardization these headings are selected from printed lists such as *Sears* or the *Library of Congress Subject Headings* list. Specialized lists also exist to give access to collections that need more detailed analysis.

CHAPTER REVIEW

Terms to understand:

closed shelves	PRECIS
fixed location	relative location
full text retrieval	specific subject entry
open shelf	thesaurus

Classification schemes:

Provide notations so that subjects can be shelved together.

DDC — numerical notation
LCC — letters and numbers

Subject headings:

Locate items individually with a specific subject entry.

Are standardized so that subjects can be gathered together in the catalog.

May be single nouns, nouns with adjectives, compound headings, or phrases, and can be subdivided for greater accuracy.

General libraries select from a general list (LCSH or Sears). Special libraries use specialized lists. Computer retrieval systems use thesauri.

PRECIS replaces subject headings with a string of relevant and connected terms. The computer selects *see* and *see also* references for these terms and produces the completed records.

CHAPTER 7

CLASSIFYING WITH DEWEY

THE DEWEY Decimal Classification (DDC) is almost synonymous with librarianship in the minds of the public. School children learn the ten classification areas and the general reader is comfortable with them. The Dewey tables are easy to work with, the scheme can be expanded to suit a collection of any size, and cataloging copy with Dewey numbers is available in many printed sources. No wonder the DDC is used all over the world and has been translated into many languages, including Chinese.

GENERAL GUIDELINES FOR CLASSIFICATION

The purpose of classification is to arrange a collection, not place a single item. Users who browse expect to find like subjects together. An efficient arrangement depends on familiarity with a collection, its contents, the reasons for its existence, and the purpose of its users.

In classification the first step is to identify the subject for the item in hand. During the technical reading the title is identified. Because it is risky to depend on the title alone in subject analysis, the table of contents and all available introductory material is examined, but catalogers rarely need to examine the entire contents of an item in order to determine a subject.

Determine where items with similar subjects have been placed in the collection by checking the catalog. The cataloger may have a choice of classification numbers, but, remembering the user, should be consistent in assigning notations.

As noted in chapter six, most items can be assigned to more than one subject heading. When an item deals with several subjects, classify under the dominant one or, when this cannot be determined, under the first mentioned in the text. When there are more than three subjects, classify under the more general topic. For example, a book of essays discussing mathematics, physics, chemistry, and biology should be classified in general science. The DDC usually gives instructions for such comprehensive works.

Never be tempted to make up a number for a subject that

is not included in the tables, because future editions may use that number for another topic. Simply use the most specific notation in the tables that covers the subject. The DDC schedules are frequently revised to reflect changes in the nature of subjects and disciplines, but cannot be completely up-to-date with current events and discoveries. New subjects are usually included in the schedules by re-assigning or expanding notations. When this happens the cataloger can decide to leave the topic in the general number, or, if a great deal of material has accumulated, to be more specific by reclassifying to the new number.

In general, the cataloger is advised to place a work where it is most useful. While the beginning cataloger may have little idea where this might be, experience with the schedules and knowledge of the collection and its users improves classification skills.

DEWEY DECIMAL CLASSIFICATION

The DDC is published in both abridged and unabridged editions. The abridged DDC shortens the numbers of the larger edition and is intended for small general collections of 20,000 items or fewer. Both editions include SCHEDULES, TABLES, and a RELATIVE INDEX. Any library, however, may house special collections that need precise subject division. In that case the notations of the unabridged edition can be used in those areas only.

Although the following discussion refers primarily to the 11th abridged edition, some examples of special uses for the 19th edition are illustrated.

DDC divides all knowledge into ten main classes. The first of the three digits indicates the class:

000	Generalities	500	Pure sciences
100	Philosophy and related disciplines	600	Technology (Applied sciences)
		700	The arts
200	Religion	800	Literature (Belles-lettres)
300	Social sciences	900	General geography and history
400	Language		

Each main class comprises ten divisions. The second digit indicates the division:

700 The arts
710   Civic & landscape art
720   Architecture
730   Plastic arts   Sculpture

740	Drawing, decorative & minor arts
750	Painting & paintings
760	Graphic arts Prints
770	Photography & photographs
780	Music
790	Recreational & performing arts

Each division has ten sections. The third digit indicates the section:

700	**The arts**
701	Philosophy & theory
702	Miscellany
703	Dictionaries & encyclopedias
704	Special topics of general applicability
705	Serial publications
706	Organizations & management
707	Study & teaching
708	Galleries, museums, art collections
709	Historical & geographical treatment

Topics are covered more specifically by subsequent divisions of the section:

750	**Painting & paintings**
751	Processes & forms
752	Color
753	Abstractions, symbolism, legend
754	Subjects of everyday life
755	Religion & religious symbolism
756	Historical events
757	Human figures & their parts
758	Other subjects
759	Historical & geographical treatment
760	**Graphic arts Prints**
761	Relief processes
762	
763	Lithographic processes
764	Serigraphy & chromolithography
765	Metal engraving
766	Mezzotinting & aquatinting processes
767	Etching & drypoint
768	
769	Prints

The blank spaces indicate that numbers included in earlier editions have been dropped from the schedule. In future editions, these numbers will be assigned to other subjects. Classification relationships change to reflect changes in knowledge itself. Each edition warns when numbers have been dropped and subjects in that section moved elsewhere in the table. The assumption is that if numbers are left vacant long enough, the existing materials will wear out, or become outdated, and when the number is used again, little material will require reclassification. Dewey once promised that numbers would be left vacant for 25 years, but that has proved impossible.

The decimal point allows numbers within a class to expand as they are further subdivided. Notice how this works in "processes and forms of painting":

751   **Processes and forms**

Class processes and forms of individual painters in 759.1–759.9

▶   **751.2–751.6 Techniques, procedures, apparatus, equipment, materials**

Class comprehensive works in 750.28

.2   **Materials**

Surfaces, pigments, mediums, fixatives, coatings

Class use of materials in specific techniques in 751.4

.3   **Apparatus, equipment, artists' models**

Class use of apparatus and equipment in specific techniques in 751.4

.4   **Techniques and procedures**

Painting with specific mediums

Including collage (with painting as the basic technique), airbrush painting

Class mosaic painting [*formerly* 751.4] in 738.5

For techniques of reproduction, see 751.5

.42   **Watercolor painting**

Do not use standard subdivisions

.45   **Oil painting**

.5   **Techniques of reproduction**

Execution, identification, determination of authenticity of reproductions, copies, forgeries, alterations

For printmaking and prints, see 760

.6   **Conservation, preservation, restoration, routine care**

Including expertizing

Class identification of reproductions, copies, forgeries, alterations in 751.5

.7   **Specific forms**

Examples: easel paintings, murals, panoramas, theatrical scenery, miniatures

Class specific subjects in specific forms in 753–758; techniques, procedures, apparatus, equipment, materials employed in specific forms in 751.2–751.6

Abridged Dewey Decimal Classification

Further subdivision of 751 from the 19th unabridged edition:

▶ **751.2–751.6 Techniques, procedures, apparatus, equipment, materials**

Class comprehensive works in 750.28

.2 **Materials**

Surfaces, pigments, mediums, fixatives, coatings

Class use of materials in specific techniques in 751.4

.3 **Apparatus, equipment, artists' models**

Class use of apparatus and equipment in specific techniques in 751.4

.4 **Techniques and procedures**

.42 Use of water-soluble mediums

For tempera painting, see 751.43

.422 Watercolor painting

Class here gouache, casein painting

.422 4 Watercolor painting techniques by subject

Add to base number 751.4224 the numbers following 704.94 in 704.942–704.949, e.g., techniques of landscape painting in watercolor 751.422436

.425 Ink painting

.425 1 Chinese

.425 2 Japanese

.426 Acrylic painting

.43 Tempera painting

.44 Fresco painting

.45 Oil painting

.454 Oil painting techniques by subject

Add to base number 751.454 the numbers following 704.94 in 704.942–704.949, e.g., techniques of landscape painting in oils 751.45436

.46 Encaustic (Wax) painting

[.48] Mosaic painting

Class in 738.5

.49 Other methods

Including finger painting, sand painting

.493 Collage

With painting as the basic technique

.494 Airbrush

Unabridged Dewey Decimal Classification

When a library has only a few items in a class, and does not plan to acquire more, it is possible to use a more general number. A special library, for example, may own only five or six books in the discipline "The Arts" and could choose to classify them all under 700. A small general collection would probably have enough materials on painting and paintings to use the number 750, which has only three subdivisions, but not the number 751. A larger collection might need to classify more precisely, using 751 for processes and forms, 755 for religious symbolism, and so forth. If the size of the collection warrants, 751 — "Processes and forms" — can be further divided by using decimals. Note that techniques of watercolor and oil painting each have their own numbers, but could be classified together under 751.4. In a large collection, users will be able to find materials more easily if the minute distinctions of the unabridged edition, which even supplies a number for finger-painting, are followed. Contrast 751.4 — "Techniques and procedures" — in the abridged edition with 751.4 — "Techniques and procedures" — in the unabridged edition, in which many more specific topics have notations created by expanding numbers.

An art library can decide to use the unabridged edition for the art materials only, but classify other subjects in the collection with the abridged edition. Special collections, in which knowledgeable users seek special information, should probably be cataloged with the unabridged edition. A collection focusing on state or local history, regardless of its size, uses the unabridged edition because it provides a specific number for each county. Classifiers are arranging materials for profitable browsing. As collections grow it is easier for users to browse when more specific numbers are used. Keep in mind shelf arrangement when classifying.

In the examples from the table, note scope notes, directions, and examples that are provided. No matter which edition of Dewey is used it is extremely important to read such material carefully and follow the instructions.

The Relative Index

After the subject of the item in hand has been identified, the class number is located. Often prepared copy and purchased cards provide numbers, and the *Sears* subject list has abridged numbers. Check the relative index and the library's shelf list before using numbers from prepared copy. This assures the number will fit the existing shelf arrangement for numbers printed on copy. The index of the DDC is called a relative index because it gives not only numbers, but also the relationships between topics.

An example from the relative index shows how aspects of a single subject, economics, may be dispersed throughout the schedules:

The history of economics is 330.9, but the economic aspects of geology are found under 553, a science notation. After selecting a possible notation from the index, check the number in the tables. If 339.5 has been tentatively selected for a book on government economic policy, turn to that number, where a SCOPE NOTE explains which topics may be placed there.

Economic	
assistance internat. *see* Foreign aid	
biology	574.6
animals	591.6
plants	581.6
botany	581.6
conditions	330.9
fluctuations	338.5
geography	330.91–.99
geology	553
growth	
macroeconomics	339.5
history	330.9
institutions	
sociology	306
order	
soc. theology	
Christianity	261.8
comp. rel.	291.1
planning	338.9
rent land econ.	333.01
resources *see* Resources	
rights	
pol. sci.	323.4
situation	330.9
stabilization	
macroeconomics	339.5
zoology	591.6

.5   **Macroeconomic policy**

Economic stabilization and growth, incomes policies, full employment policies; use of fiscal policy, e.g., government spending, budget surpluses and deficits, taxation; use of monetary policy, e.g., discount rates offered by central banks, reserve requirements imposed on banks, open market operations, regulation of bank credit

Including income redistribution, transfer payments

Class measures to combat inflation in 332.4, to control economic fluctuations in 338.5, to promote growth and development in 338.9

Note that measures to combat inflation are not classed in this number but in 332.4. Never attempt to classify from the index alone; always check the tables and read all scope notes.

Classification is generally by subject, but within subjects certain sub-arrangements are possible. These sub-arrangements are presented in auxiliary tables. There are four such tables in the abridged edition:

Auxiliary Tables

Table 1: standard subdivisions
Table 2: areas

Table 3: subdivisions of individual literatures
Table 4: subdivisions of individual languages

Table 3 is used only with the 800s (literature) and table 4 with the 400s (language).

The notations in Table 1, STANDARD SUBDIVISIONS, may be added to any DDC number unless directions explicitly state: "Do not use standard subdivisions."

SUMMARY

—01 Philosophy and theory
—02 Miscellany
—03 Dictionaries, encyclopedias, concordances
—04 Special topics of general applicability
—05 Serial publications
—06 Organizations and management
—07 Study and teaching
—09 Historical and geographical treatment

Suppose that a book on government economic policy is a book of definitions of terms. The notation tentatively chosen for that topic is 339.5. To group dictionaries together within the topic the number can be expanded with the standard subdivision number 03, forming the notation 339.503.

If the work is a history of macroeconomic policy the notation is 339.509. Standard subdivisions are indicated with a zero. Unless directed, do not use more than one, no matter where the decimal point falls. For example the correct notation for how to teach science is 507 *not* 500.7 or 500.07. How to teach science of the earth is 550.7 *not* 550.07.

One of the most commonly used standard subdivisions is 09, which denotes historical and geographical treatment of a subject. To indicate a biography, the number should be lengthened to 092.

Biographies can be classified in a separate section, or placed with related subject matter. The second practice is followed at the Library of Congress and many academic libraries, where a biography of Queen Victoria would be found in English history, a biography of Hank Aaron in the baseball section, and a biography of a surgeon in the medical area. Public libraries have customarily marked biographies with a B and shelved them in a general biography section. This would probably not be a good policy in a collection that serves many kinds of research needs. A student writing on the unification of Germany would expect to find biographies of Bismarck with German history, and a reader with an interest in the French Revolution will look for biographies of the famous participants among other works on the subject. Similarly, high school students who want to read about tennis stars will be better served when these books are shelved with other tennis books, rather than scattered through the general biography section. A biography should not be routinely assigned to one general section, however. For example, 792 is the notation for Theater (stage presentations). Biographies of famous theater personalities arranged under 792.092 are easily found. This method of arrangement does not preclude maintaining a general biography section containing biographies for recreational reading.

Sometimes the coverage of a topic may be limited to a single geographical area. If the collection contains a great deal of material on a particular subject, the cataloger may decide to subdivide the subject by place using the AREA TABLES.

Area Tables

Table 2. Areas

SUMMARY

—1   Areas, regions, places in general
—2   Persons regardless of area, region, place
—3   The ancient world
—4   Europe   Western Europe
—5   Asia   Orient   Far East
—6   Africa
—7   North America
—8   South America
—9   Other parts of world and extraterrestrial worlds   Pacific Ocean islands (Oceania)

The schedules often give the instruction "add area notations." When there are no such instructions, area notations may still be added by placing 09 from Table 1 in front of the area number. Suppose the collection contains many items concerning the macroeconomic policies of governments. These can be arranged by regions. Because there are no directions at 339.5 about using area codes, 09 will be used with the proper notations.

macroeconomic policy in Japan   339.5 macroeconomic policy
339.50952   09   standard subdivision
                             52   area number for Japan

When instructions read "add area" notation, as they do at

549.9 (geographical distribution of minerals) the area number is added directly to the class number 549.9. For example, geographical distribution of minerals in Japan is 549.952.

Table 3
and Table 4

Table 3 applies only to the literature schedule and is used with numbers 810-890. This table divides literature collections according to their form. Table 4, for the language schedule, is used with numbers 420-490 and, within particular languages, distinguishes between dictionaries, grammars, and readers.

Language
and Literature
(including fiction)
Tables

Although the disciplines of language and literature are closely related, these two areas are widely separated on the shelves in the DDC system. The 400s and the 800s are structured in much the same way, however, and both contain MNEMONIC DEVICES to assist classification and shelf location. Note that the second digit in the number denotes the same language in either class, and that, in the subdivisions, the third digit denotes the literary form.

Summary of the Two General Classes

400	**Language**	**800**	**Literature (Belles-lettres)**
410	Linguistics	810	American literature in English
420	English & Anglo-Saxon languages	820	English & Anglo-Saxon literatures
430	Germanic languages German	830	Literatures of Germanic languages
440	Romance languages French	840	Literatures of Romance languages
450	Italian, Romanian, Rhaeto-Romanic	850	Italian, Romanian, Rhaeto-Romanic
460	Spanish & Portuguese languages	860	Spanish & Portuguese literatures
470	Italic languages Latin	870	Italic literatures Latin
480	Hellenic Classical Greek	880	Hellenic literatures Greek
490	Other languages	890	Literatures of other languages

Subdivisions

420	**English & Anglo-Saxon languages**	**430**	**Germanic languages German**
421	Written & spoken English	431	Written & spoken German
422	English etymology	432	German etymology
423	English dictionaries	433	German dictionaries
424		434	
425	English structural system	435	German structural system
426		436	
427	Nonstandard English	437	Nonstandard German
428	Standard English usage	438	Standard German usage
429	Anglo-Saxon (Old English)	439	Other Germanic languages

820	English & Anglo-Saxon literatures	830	Literatures of Germanic languages
821	English poetry	831	German poetry
822	English drama	832	German drama
823	English fiction	833	German fiction
824	English essays	834	German essays
825	English speeches	835	German speeches
826	English letters	836	German letters
827	English satire & humor	837	German satire & humor
828	English miscellaneous writings	838	German miscellaneous writings
829	Anglo-Saxon (Old English)	839	Other Germanic literatures

The first number indicates discipline:

4 = Language   8 = Literature

The second number indicates nationality:

42 = Language   English & Anglo-Saxon
82 = Literature   English & Anglo-Saxon

The third number indicates form:

423 = Language   English dictionaries
823 = Literature   English fiction

To use the tables in either section, first locate the BASE NUMBER in the schedules.

The base number is made up of the number indicating discipline and the number indicating language, and is identified from the schedules. Once the base number is located turn to the proper table — e.g. Table 4 for the 400s and Table 3 for the eight hundreds — to find the correct notation for form.

To classify a book of humorous stories in German:

Literature

Base number for German = 83
Table 3 - satire and humor collections of more than one author = 7008
Added to the base number = 837.008

Language

A graded German reader would be classified in the 400s from the schedule:
Base number - German language = 43
From the tables:
Readers (graded selection) = 86
A graded German reader = 438.6

In most libraries the 400 section, even including the dictionaries, is a small section. Classification can probably be done from the general schedules without expanding the tables. The literature section, the 800s, is much larger, more complicated to arrange, and requires more attention.

The 800s reflect certain of Dewey's assumptions, as do other sections. He assumed that the major literatures of the world had been identified and could be conveniently arranged between 810-880, leaving 890 for other national literatures that might appear. This has led to the present situation in the abridged DDC, in which the literature of more than 70 languages is crowded between 890 and 899. In this span the system of base numbers breaks down, and only a base number for Russian is identified — 891.7. A large literature collection is better arranged using the unabridged edition.

Literature
Shelf
Arrangement

Dewey also envisioned fiction shelved in the 800s, according to language of composition, and provided the form digit 3 for this. Most libraries, however, prefer to classify fiction separately with F or Fic used in place of a DDC number. This normally works quite well. Some fictional works, however, are better classed in the DDC numbers. An example is fiction written in a language other than English. The patron looking for a novel in German or Italian should not have to search the entire fiction section, but only among novels in those languages. It is more convenient to place novels written in French in 843 than somewhere in F. High school and college libraries can also consider placing study texts of novels in the 800 classification, because these are not suitable for casual reading, but are intended for the literature student. This number can also be considered for biographies of novelists, adding, of course, 092. A biography of Hemingway would therefore be shelved 813.092. A critical analysis of Hemingway's novels would also be shelved in 813. A library could choose to put popular editions of Hemingway's novels in the F section, but critical analysis and study editions of the works in 813 beside those books concerned with his life. This arrangement places works logically for users. Although separated on the shelves, Hemingway materials are still related in the catalog under the access point for Hemingway.

Although Shakespeare has his own notation (822.3), shelving the vast amount of material concerning this author is a problem even in small collections. The unabridged DDC has a table for arranging the works of Shakespeare which can be adapted for use with any author and could be used with the abridged edition as a guide for shelving Shakespeare and other writers. A work dealing with authorship controversies would be 822.3A; a biography of Shakespeare, 822.3B. Literary criticism of the poet T. S. Eliot would be 821E; his poetry would be shelved in 821I or 821J.

William Shakespeare

If desired, subarrange works about and by Shakespeare according to the following table, which may be adapted for use with any specific author:

A   Authorship controversies
       (It is optional to class here bibliography; prefer 016.82233)

B   Biography

D   Critical appraisal
       Class critical appraisal of individual works in O-Z

E   Textual criticism
       Class textual criticism of individual works in O-Z

F   Sources, allusions, learning

G   Societies, concordances, miscellany

H   Quotations, condensations, adaptations

I   Complete works in English without notes

J   Complete works in English with notes

K   Complete works in translation

L   Partial collections in English without notes

M   Partial collections in English with notes

N   Partial collections in translation

▶O-Z   Individual works

Even when all fiction is separated in "Fic" it is often necessary to subdivide it further. Many readers enjoy short stories, but would not want to browse the whole fiction section to find them. Short stories can be shelved separately, marked S.C. for Story Collection, or given a DDC number and shelved with other literary forms. Fiction is more often selected by browsing than non-fiction. Some patrons want only mysteries, others only romance. Special fiction collections in such popular subjects can be maintained for those readers.

General History and Geography

900	General geography & history		940	General history of Europe	
910	General geography	Travel	941	British Isles	
920	General biography & genealogy		942	England & Wales	
930	General history of ancient world		943	Central Europe	Germany
940	General history of Europe		944	France & Monaco	
950	General history of Asia		945	Italy	
960	General history of Africa		946	Iberian Peninsula	Spain
970	General history of North America		947	Soviet Union	
980	General history of South America		948	Scandinavia	
990	General history of other areas		949	Other parts of Europe	

910	General geography	Travel
911	Historical geography	
912	Graphic representations of earth	
913	Geography of ancient world	
914	Europe	
915	Asia	
916	Africa	
917	North America	
918	South America	
919	Other areas & worlds	

The 900 section is not as complex as the 800s, but it is also a large area, and concepts used in the 800s to save space in the schedules are also employed here. Again, the first step is identifying the subject, whether history as a discipline (900-909) or geography as a discipline (910-912) or general geography (913-919) or general history (930-999).

Summary—from Table 2. Areas

-41 British Isles
-42 England and Wales
-43 Central Europe   Germany
-44 France and Monaco
-45 Italy
-46 Iberian Peninsula and adjacent islands   Spain
-47 Union of Soviet Socialist Republics (Soviet Union)
-48 Scandinavia
-49 Other parts of Europe

Any work that deals with geography and travel in the ancient and modern world can be classified using the base number 91 and the correct notation from Table 2, the area notation table. If the approach is historical, rather than geographical, the base number is 9 plus the correct notation from area 2. A travel book entitled *What's Doing in England* is assigned 914.2 whereas a history of England is 942.

The history section will usually be much larger than the geography section and must be subdivided by historical periods if users are to browse with ease. United States history (973) is subdivided by chronological periods, and after the 20th century, by terms of individual presidents; e.g. 973.924 is President Nixon, 973.925 is Ford, and 973.926 is Carter. The current edition lists no notation for President Reagan's administration but the correct one can easily be added. Since this span to 973.999 may be used for individual presidents, catalogers need not worry about running out of notations until the 22nd century.

There is a close connection between history and biography, for a biography is a history of an individual. The 900 schedule provides a span for classification of biography, both general and specific. In reality, few libraries use this span [920-928] preferring either to mark the materials "B," or classify with a specific discipline using the standard subdivision notation 092.

Each library decides how to arrange its collection to make it accessible to patrons. Decisions on where to shelve biographies, how to arrange fiction, and how closely to classify vary from institution to institution, and the DDC schedules themselves do not address these problems. Once a library has established policies the cataloger should have little difficulty in applying any section of the DDC correctly, provided that all scope notes and directions are carefully followed.

Selecting a DDC classification notation does not complete the call number. A number of items may share a classification number, depending on which subjects are in the collection. In general, a BOOK NUMBER is used to achieve alphabetical arrangement within the classification. Most libraries try to assign a unique call number to each item. The call number is made up of a classification number and a book number whose notation is based on the main entry. Materials are shelved alphabetically according to main entry (excluding articles if a title) or, in the case of biographies, the subject's last name, thus assuring that works about people will be found together. Call numbers are recorded in the catalog and are marked on the item where they can be seen by the patron; for example, on the spine of a book. Many libraries simply add the first three letters of the main entry, or subject, or author's name underneath the classification to create the call number. Large collections may use a Cutter "author table" to provide a letter number combination book number. These tables were first developed by Charles Cutter and later revised by Kate Sanborn to supply book numbers for the DDC. These tables are alphabetical arrangements by name or a shortened form of the name, each with a number behind it. For example, the name Groff will be found in a long list of Gs with the number 893 beside it. The Cutter number for Groff will be G893 and would be added beneath a DDC number to form a call number.

BOOK NUMBERS

Gro	89
Grobe	891
Groco	892
Groff	893
Groh	894
Groll	895
Grolm	896
Gromi	897
Grone	898
Groom	899
Gyo	998

DDC number 973 call number
      G893 Cutter table

973 call number
GRO using first 3
letters of
main entry

A CUTTER TABLE is simple to use and keeps a collection in excellent order. It will take longer to look up names in the table, however, than it will to use the first three letters only. Cutter never envisioned that many works would be entered by title, but today title main entry is common. It is difficult, but not impossible, to use the table with other than proper names. Although use of the Cutter tables may take longer initially, it can save shelving time.

Each library must decide whether it would be feasible to use staff time to create an alphabetical shelf order. In a small collection a classification number may be enough, especially for non-fiction. Even in a small library, however, fiction is another matter, and these materials are often not kept in good order, even when marked with three letters. Cutter may be used only with fiction, which is normally shelved by author anyway. More markings can be added as desired; for example, an author's novels can be kept in alphabetical order by title by adding lower-case letters to the book number.

Hemingway — For Whom the Bell Tolls	H375f
The Sun Also Rises	H375s

Some libraries mark fiction with the entire last name of the author on the spine to insure correct shelving. Publication date can be added below for clarification.

In research libraries many users search in the catalog and then on the shelf for a specific work. In large collections, an item marked with only three letters might be difficult to find. In such cases a unique call number is extremely important and time should be taken to provide one. If a collection is very small and will probably remain so, or if material is mainly located by browsing, any system that provides a rough alphabetical order may be sufficient.

RECLASSIFICATION   One limitation of a classification scheme based on the present state of knowledge is that knowledge changes, grows, and shifts emphasis. Such a scheme will soon cease to reflect what people are studying, reading, watching, or acquiring for libraries. The scheme of knowledge outlined in the first DDC tables (1876) has been thoroughly superseded and in each subsequent edition topics have been relocated, discontinued, expanded, or even created anew in PHOENIX SCHEDULES. Dewey assumed that the major disciplines were established for all time, and so used all the numbers in his schedules without planning for expansion. The problem is evident in each section and can be easily understood by looking at the 100s and 200s.

In the 1870s psychology was hardly acknowledged as a field of study and Dewey allowed it only one span of numbers. The rest of the 100s was taken up with philosophy. Contemporary librarians need the imbalance reversed to reflect the contents of their collections. In the 11th abridged edition the 150s take up one third of the entire 100 schedule.

Dewey assumed that by leaving 290 for religions other than Christianity he had provided as many spans as any library would need. As a result the present abridged edition assigns ten specific religions and all religions of Black Africa, and of Native American origin to 299.

100	Philosophy & related disciplines
110	Metaphysics
120	Epistemology, causation, humankind
130	Paranormal phenomena & arts
140	Specific philosophical viewpoints
150	Psychology
160	Logic
170	Ethics (Moral philosophy)
180	Ancient, medieval, Oriental
190	Modern Western philosophy
200	**Religion**
210	Natural religion
220	Bible
230	Christian theology
240	Christian moral & devotional
250	Local church & religious orders
260	Social & ecclesiastical theology
270	History & geography of church
280	Christian denominations & sects
290	Other & comparative religions

Successive editors of the DDC have tried to produce schedules that reflect current needs. At present a new edition is prepared every seven years. Without exception, each edition makes a great many changes, presenting the cataloger with the problem of whether to reclassify every time DDC changes numbers.

Reclassification is not a job to undertake lightly because hours must be spent changing the notation in every place that it appears. Some librarians are vociferous in their opposition to reclassification, claiming it is not worth the time or money to shift items on a shelf. This school of thought adopts an edition of Dewey and sticks with it. At the other end of the spectrum are those who feel it necessary to reclassify with each edition in order to keep classification consistent with current knowledge. Most librarians take a middle course, perhaps classifying new arrivals according to the latest edition, but not reclassifying older material. This means users will not be able to browse easily for a while, but eventually much of the material in the older section can be discarded, and the remainder reclassified. Others might ignore minor changes, but reclassify when a major relocation or a Phoenix schedule appears. Reclassification is a decision that is made by weighing available resources against the needs of users.

SUMMARY

When catalogers choose main and added entries, they are influenced by the desire to standardize the identification of items from library to library. However, DDC notations are chosen so that an individual collection can be arranged to support the needs of the users, whether they require research materials or a good mystery. Large, specialized, or research libraries rely on the unabridged DDC for precise classification, whereas small general libraries with less than 20,000 items will find the more general numbers in the abridged edition adequate. Even a small library may need precise classification for specialized collections, and it is appropriate to employ the unabridged edition when preparing these materials.

Locating subject notations in DDC is not difficult, but it is important to read and follow the directions. Consult the index, find a number in the schedule, and check the shelf list to insure that like subjects will be found together on the shelf. Certain subarrangements can be achieved within the subject area by using the auxiliary tables. Again, it is extremely important to follow the directions when subdividing.

Certain decisions about classification remain for the cataloger. These are made on the basis of the "convenience of the public," which in the case of classification is their browsing convenience. There are, for example, various options when classing biographies and fiction. Because the literature section houses such diverse materials it can be confusing to arrange, and some logical shelving scheme has to be worked out. Book numbers must be added to the DDC to complete call numbers and to achieve alphabetical order on the shelf. Achieving perfect order requires time; the librarian balances time available against the requirements for order.

No classification system is perfect, and librarians have limited resources and time. Yet bringing order out of the chaotic world of information is one of the most important responsibilities of the profession and classification can be a key to fulfilling it.

CHAPTER REVIEW

Terms to understand:

area table	scope note
base number	Phoenix schedule
book number	standard subdivision
Cutter table	relative index
mnenomic devices	schedules

Classification:

Be consistent.
Follow a schedule.

Dewey Decimal Classification:

Abridged — for small general collections.
Unabridged — for large collections or in-depth collections.

Consult the relative index, find the notation in the schedules, carefully read scope notes and directions. Check catalog.

Policies determined by each library:

How to class biographies.
How to arrange the literature section.
Assignment of book numbers.
When to reclassify.

CHAPTER 8

PROVIDING SUBJECT ACCESS

CLASSIFICATION gives an item a shelf address, locating it among other materials within the same general subject. Catalogers then provide fine-tuned content access by assigning subject headings. A title can have only one shelf location, but can be accessed in the catalog via as many subject headings as the cataloger chooses.

The assignment of both subject headings and classification notations depends on the content of the material. During the technical reading, consider the intellectual content with both processes in mind. The main thrust of the work determines shelf location and suggests a subject heading. Additional topics or aspects indicate further access points for catalog retrieval. The subject headings selected should both lead to the appropriate specific titles in the collection, and serve as a gathering device for all titles dealing with similar topics. To do this successfully, headings have to be uniformly applied and a standard list consulted. *Sears* and the *Library of Congress Subject Headings* (LCSH) are the lists most commonly used for general collections. As no one can predict exactly what topics a user will search out, i.e., cars or automobiles; flying saucers or UFO's; drug habit or drug abuse, these standard lists provide a network of terms and are laced with cross references guiding to those uniform headings preferred for use.

SEARS AND LCSH

Organization
and
Arrangement

Each of the subject heading tools lists topics alphabetically with WORD-BY-WORD FILING. In *Sears* the preferred headings appear in bold-face print. Terms not used appear in ordinary print, followed by a cross reference to the approved uniform term (See Figure 8-1).

Sears, the less complex tool, provides fewer and less complicated terms and is preferred for small general libraries. LCSH is more complex because it expands topic areas into many subdivisions and includes numerous proper nouns as topics (Bergen-op-Zoom). Terms are coordinated between the two so that most major headings are identical. Both use automobiles, not cars or some other equivalent term. Under some circumstances a specialized library might apply LCSH head-

SEARS

Drug addiction.   *See* **Drug abuse; Narcotic habit**
Drug addicts.   *See* **Narcotic addicts**
Drug habit.   *See* **Drug abuse; Narcotic habit**
Drug pushers.   *See* **Narcotic traffic**
Drug therapy.   *See* **Chemotherapy**
Drug traffic.   *See* **Narcotic traffic**
Drug use.   *See* **Drug abuse**; and classes of people with the subdivision *Drug use,* e.g. **Criminals—Drug use; Youth—Drug use;** etc.

LCSH

Drugs, Antitubercular
  See Antitubercular agents
Drugs, Antitussive
  See Antitussive agents
Drugs, Antiviral
  See Antiviral agents
Drugs, Bronchoconstrictor
  See Bronchoconstrictor agents
Drugs, Bronchodilator
  See Bronchodilator agents

Figure 8-1

Compare the treatment of alcoholism in *Sears* and LCSH.

SEARS

Alcoholism   616.86

Use chiefly for medical materials, including works on drunkenness, dipsomania, etc.

See also **Alcohol—Physiological effect; Alcoholics; Liquor problems; Temperance;** also classes of people with the subdivision *Alcohol use,* e.g. **Youth—Alcohol use;** etc.

x Dipsomania; Drinking; Drunkenness; Intemperance; Intoxication

xx **Alcohol; Drug abuse; Liquor prcblem; Temperance**

LCSH

Alcoholism   *(Indirect)   (Disease, RC565; Temperance, HV5001-5720)*

Used chiefly for medical works; includes works on drunkenness, dipsomania, etc.

The general heading for works on the temperance question is Temperance, under which are entered books on the temperance movement, popular and controversial works, and fiction. Under Liquor problem are entered works of an administrative or local character. Liquor traffic is used for the liquor industry, Liquor laws for the legal side of the question, and Liquors for the technical side. Special topics, *e.g.* Local option, Gothenburg system, Prohibition, License system, take special headings.

sa Alcohol and children
  Alcohol and Jews
  Alcohol and the aged
  Alcohol and the clergy
  Alcohol and women
  Alcohol and youth
  Alcoholics
  Children of alcoholic parents
  Korsakoff's syndrome
  subdivision Alcohol use *under names of ethnic groups and classes of persons, e.g.* Spanish Americans in the United States—Alcohol use
x Alcohol intoxication

  Dipsomania
  Drunkenness
  Inebriety
  Intemperance
  Intoxication
xx Alcohol
  Drug abuse
  Liquor problem
  Temperance
Notes under Liquor laws; Liquor problem; Liquor traffic; Liquors; Prohibition; Temperance
— Complications and sequelae
— Physiological aspects
    See Alcohol—Physiological effect
— Prevention
— — Finance
      sa Federal aid to alcoholism programs
— Psychological aspects
    See Alcoholics—Psychology
— Punched card systems
    See Punched card systems—Alcohol
— Study and teaching   *(Indirect)*
    x Alcohol education
      Alcoholism education
      Temperance—Study and teaching
— Treatment   *(Indirect)*
    sa Alcoholics—Hospitals and asylums
      Alcoholism counseling
    x Keeley cure

Figure 8-2

ings for its main collection and use *Sears* for any small general area. Libraries can readily replace *Sears* with LCSH as their holdings grow. Both tools can be used interchangeably with DDC and LC classification, although *Sears* is commonly associated with Dewey and LCSH with LC.

Note that the scope note provided in both lists indicates that alcoholism is a subject heading chiefly for medical works. LCSH headings expand this topic area considerably, providing a number of subdivisions (indicated by hyphens: alcoholism-mortality) and combined terms (alcohol and children).

Each list also provides a general classification number next to major terms (some earlier editions of *Sears* omitted this, but it has now been reinstated). Studying these numbers can aid in the selection of subject headings by helping place a particular heading in the general scheme of knowledge. For example, the *Sears* heading DECISION MAKING is rather vague, but the addition of two DDC numbers, 153.8 and 658.4, indicate that it can be used for materials in psychology, or in the general management area. When necessary, use the DDC numbers in *Sears* to aid the interpretation of the subject heading.

Both lists are arranged by the same general principles, but regardless of which is ultimately consulted, the introduction to *Sears* — "Principles of the *Sears List of Subject Headings*" — is essential reading for the beginner. Follow the same general process of assigning subject headings no matter which subject heading tool is employed. During the technical reading note the contents of the material by examining the Table of Contents, skimming all introductory material, and dipping into the text. Form a general idea of where the contents fit into the classification scheme. Establish a tentative notation and headings by consulting the cataloging tools. Then, if necessary, check the shelf list and the catalog before making a firm decision. After the call number is established and subject headings assigned, select the cross references to complete the process.

USING SEARS

Sears, intended to be a working record, leaves one half of each page blank for the addition of such local topics and proper noun subjects as are assigned in individual libraries. Created for collections of less than 50,000 items, *Sears* provides terms in common American usage, rather than scientific or technical language. Space is saved by not listing every possible term, but by giving general permission to add certain categories of headings as needed. These include common names, such as flower or animal names, proper names, and corporate bodies. When in doubt about the correct form to use for a name or corporate body follow the rules in AACR2. Space is also saved by "key" headings which serve as models for subdivision of unlisted terms:

any president	PRESIDENT—U.S.
any author	SHAKESPEARE, WILLIAM
countries	UNITED STATES
states	OHIO
municipalities	CHICAGO
language	ENGLISH LANGUAGE
literature	ENGLISH LITERATURE
wars	WORLD WAR 1939-1945

Besides these, other general lists of subdivisions are provided in the preface and may be added to headings as needed; for example, SCIENCE—DICTIONARIES. These subdivisions are generally a form of publication such as maps, bibliographies, charts, encyclopedias, periodicals, etc.

When a subject heading is assigned from these general, unlisted categories, this decision must be recorded, just as when a decision is made about the form of a proper name. With *Sears,* however, no separate authority file is necessary, for the blank half of each page is intended for this purpose. Record the decision by writing the heading in proper alphabetical order, on the right-hand side of the page. Maintain these records carefully, for they make *Sears* a useful working tool for an individual collection.

First turn to a general term suggested by the content. Often help will appear at this point in the form of a scope note giving a general definition of the content appropriate for this heading.

ASSIGNING
HEADINGS

After the scope note are listed several *see also* headings, which are related and usually more specific. Consider whether any of these is more appropriate for the work being cataloged. If for example (in Figure 8-3) CHILDREN—COSTUME might be a more accurate heading, turn to that place and read the scope note to see if it is appropriate.

If a decision is made to stay with Costume, and if that heading has never been used in the catalog before, this decision is recorded by making a check mark against the heading.

✓ Costume 391; 792

Costume   391
>
> Use for descriptive and historical materials on the costume of particular countries or periods and for materials on fancy costume and theatrical costumes. Materials dealing with clothing from a practical standpoint, including the art of dress, are entered under **Clothing and dress.** Materials describing the prevailing mode or style in dress are entered under **Fashion**
>
> *See also*

Arms and armor	**Hats**
Clothing and dress	**Makeup, Theatrical**
Cosmetics	**Millinery**
Fans	**Uniforms, Military**
Fashion	**Wigs**

> *also* classes of people with the subdivision *Costume,* e.g. **Children—Costume;** etc.
>
> *x* Acting—Costume; Fancy dress; Style in dress; Theatrical costume
>
> *xx* **Clothing and dress; Ethnology; Fashion; Manners and customs**

Figure 8-3

Children—Costume   391
> Use for descriptive and historical materials on children's costume among various nations and at different periods. Materials dealing with children's clothing from a practical standpoint are entered under **Children's clothing**

Figure 8-4

The cataloger of course is not limited to the term Costume because, at least in theory, any number of subject entries can be added for any one item. In practice, three specific subject headings are normally sufficient. Do not assign both a general and a specific subject heading for the same work. For example, FANS, HATS, and COSTUME should not be assigned to one item. Always be specific, and remember that in many cases a single subject heading can represent the entire contents of an item as accurately as is possible. Cross references can then be added to guide users to that term. It is not obligatory to give each item a subject heading. If the content is vague and no specific subject can be found do not assign one.

CROSS
REFERENCES

Because users may not think of the term Costume when searching for this topic, but look for Theatrical Costume or Fashion instead, a network of cross references is built to help locate the correct heading. The decision to use the subject heading COSTUME is recorded in *Sears* and also added to the catalog record itself in the tracings. The record of the cross references created is, however, recorded only in *Sears*.

It is impossible to predict all the terms a user might think of trying, but *Sears* does provide the more obvious ones. Drop down to the single "x" term under Costume.

Costume   391

> Use for descriptive and historical materials on the costume of particular countries or periods and for materials on fancy costume and theatrical costumes. Materials dealing with clothing from a practical standpoint, including the art of dress, are entered under **Clothing and dress.** Materials describing the prevailing mode or style in dress are entered under **Fashion**
>
> *See also*

Arms and armor	**Hats**
Clothing and dress	**Makeup, Theatrical**
Cosmetics	**Millinery**
Fans	**Uniforms, Military**
Fashion	**Wigs**

> *also* classes of people with the subdivision *Costume,*
> e.g. **Children—Costume;** etc.
>
> x Acting—Costume; Fancy dress; Style in dress; Single "x" terms
> Theatrical costume ————————
>
> xx **Clothing and dress; Ethnology; Fashion; Man-**
> **ners and customs** ——————————— Double "xx" terms

Figure 8-5

These terms are those that are *not* used. Anyone who looks up Acting—Costume, for example, finds a *see* reference sending them to the assigned term Costume. Make such a reference only when it is likely that a user would look for a particular term. *See* references will direct users from terms unused in the catalog to correct terms—in this case, Costume.

```
            Fancy Dress

                see

          COSTUME
```

Check each term having a *see* reference under Costume; then turn to the unused terms in alphabetical sequence and check them also.

x Acting—Costume; Fancy dress; Style in dress; Theatrical costume

Famines—United States 904
   x United States—Famines
Fancy dress. *See* **Costume**
Fans 391
   xx **Costume**
Fantastic fiction 808.3; Fic
   See also **Science fiction**
   xx **Fiction**

Figure 8-6

Rather than thinking of inappropriate terms, users may think of subjects too general for their precise needs. In these cases, the "xx" (*see also*) references can be helpful. These "xx" terms are related to broader terms. For example, users might search under CLOTHING AND DRESS when material on Costume is more directly related to their needs. These "xx" (*see also*) references can be used to guide users to more specific headings.

```
        Clothing and Dress

              See also

        Costume
```

Make a check mark in front of any "xx" term used. Then, to complete the record, check any *see also* references made under Clothing and Dress.

See also **Children's clothing; Costume; Dress accessories; Dressmaking; Fashion; Men's clothing; Tailoring; Women's clothing;** etc.; also names of articles of clothing and accessories, e.g. **Buttons; Hats; Hosiery; Leather garments; Shoes and shoe industry;** etc.

xx **Clothing and dress; Ethnology; Fashion; Manners and customs**

Figure 8-7

In the case of Clothing and Dress another type of *see also* is possible — a general reference:

```
          Clothing and Dress

             see also names of

        Articles of clothing and accessories
        e.g., BUTTONS
```

Cross references send users to the heading assigned for the material in hand. Since it would make little sense to send users away, all cross references made for a work on Costume send users to that term, which will always appear after any *see* or *see also* reference that has been made.

The decision to make a cross reference is made by each library. After cross references are in place there is no means of knowing whether they are helping users or confusing them. Make only those references that will lead users to specific items owned. Once a network of references is in place in the catalog, it need never be added again. When *Sears* is faithfully checked, the cataloger is instantly aware that appropriate cross references exist in the catalog for every work that is added.

SPECIFIC SUBJECT AREAS

Assigning subject headings for language and literature, and geography and history, requires as much thought and attention as does classification in those areas. Dewey provides area tables for both language and literature and divides geography from history. History is shelved by periods. *Sears* provides language and literature models for assigning subject headings and divides geography and history in much the same way as Dewey.

When assigning subject headings in the areas of language and literature the emphasis is normally not on the subject of the content, but on the language and form. The *Sears* list reflects this by providing headings indicating whether a work is a Greek or Latin dictionary, an American play or a British novel. By using the subject heading "English language" as a model the cataloger can assign headings for works dealing with various aspects of any language.

LANGUAGE AND
LITERATURE

101

FRENCH LANGUAGE – DICTIONARIES
RUSSIAN LANGUAGE – HISTORY
JAPANESE LANGUAGE – PRONUNCIATION

It is important to know the language in which a work of literature is written, but here the situation is more complex. COLLECTIVE WORKS may contain either works of literature or critical discussions of those works.

"English literature" and its subdivisions serve as the model heading:

English literature   820
    Subdivisions used under this heading may be used under
    other literatures.

Two subdivisions are especially useful. The one used for collective works:

ENGLISH LITERATURE – COLLECTIONS

and the one used for critical works:

ENGLISH LITERATURE – HISTORY AND CRITICISM

Use the entire subdivision "history and criticism" to identify criticism of single works, such as HAMLET – HISTORY AND CRITICISM; or of a literary form, i.e., FRENCH DRAMA – HISTORY AND CRITICISM.

Assign no subject heading for works written by an individual author. The user searches either under the author's name, i.e., Miller, Arthur, or the title, *Death of a Salesman*. Added headings are unnecessary.

Assigning subject headings for fiction can be as confusing as providing a classification number. The heading FICTION is used only for works dealing with fiction as a literary form. HISTORICAL FICTION only for materials about historical fiction. SCIENCE FICTION, however, leads the user to science fiction novels. There is a heading SEA STORIES provided for fictional works dealing with the sea, but someone interested in reading a historical novel finds this form in the catalog by the circuitous route of locating a subject heading indicating a historical period – for example, U.S. – HISTORY – CIVIL WAR, 1861-1865 – and checking to see if "Fiction" has been added as a subdivision. Fiction as a subdivision can be added to any subject heading when appropriate, OLD AGE – FICTION. However, many libraries choose to add no subject headings at all to fictional works, reasoning that patrons will use the catalog to find some titles, but frequently select materials by browsing. Some libraries try to facilitate this browsing by creating separate sections for historical fiction or mystery stories. This method also has drawbacks, because it becomes more difficult to locate individual works when they are separated from the general fiction collection.

Another type of literature that may cause confusion in assigning subject headings is biography. Works discussing biography as a literary form are assigned the heading:

BIOGRAPHY (AS A LITERARY FORM)

This will be a relatively small amount of material. Works recounting the lives of people, either individually or collectively, are more numerous and in far greater demand.

For the life of an individual the only subject heading absolutely necessary is the name of that person, inverted, and written in capitals at the top of the card: NIGHTINGALE, FLORENCE. If there is doubt about which form of the name to use, consult AACR2 or the name authority file and record the decision in *Sears*. The Library of Congress often assigns additional subject headings to biographical works and might add NURSES AND NURSING or GREAT BRITAIN – HISTORY – CRIMEAN WAR, 1853-1856 to a biography of Miss Nightingale. Normally this is not necessary. Make such headings only when a biography contains so much information about a field it is also a useful reference for the topic. For example, a biography of Marie Antoinette could be assigned an additional subject heading, FRANCE – HISTORY – REVOLUTION – 1789-1799. Do not do this as a matter of course, only when it is warranted by the contents.

Normally, the subdivision "biography" is never used after an individual name, but there can be exceptions. When there is voluminous material about an individual, it is necessary to use certain subdivisions after the name. The model SHAKESPEARE, WILLIAM shows such examples: SHAKESPEARE, WILLIAM – BIBLIOGRAPHY; SHAKESPEARE, WILLIAM – ADAPTATIONS; or SHAKESPEARE, WILLIAM – BIOGRAPHY. Otherwise use biography only as a subdivision for collective biographies – those works that contain biographies of more than three individuals. When these collective biographies are organized by place, the place may be the subject heading, subdivided by biography.

Title - LIVES OF FAMOUS ROMANS
Subject heading - ROME – BIOGRAPHY

When they are organized by class of person and there is

103

no adequate term to describe its members, use the subject in general, subdivided by biography:

Title — GREAT QUARTERBACKS OF THE NFL
Subject heading - FOOTBALL–BIOGRAPHY

Otherwise, enter under terms such as

ARTISTS, SPIES, DICTATORS

and do not add the subdivision biography.

Geography and History

The name of any geographical area or place—country, state, city, or other unit—may be used as a subject heading in *Sears*. These geographic units can be made more specific by adding subject subdivisions. Likewise, certain subjects, whose treatment is limited to a particular locality, can be made more specific by subdividing by geographical unit.

Dewey makes provisions for locating materials by place with the addition of an area notation, and when this option is employed, specific directions in the schedules are carefully followed. *Sears* also permits place to be added, and here too directions must be carefully observed. Unlike Dewey, *Sears* sometimes directs that place will come first, followed by subject. At other times subject is divided by place. If it is important to indicate place in a subject heading, consult *Sears* for the correct procedure.

Sometimes directions for adding place will be found with the subject headings as illustrated in the following examples found in *Sears*:

Socialism (may subdiv. geog.)   320.5; 335

A general directive that this subject heading may be divided by any area unit the cataloger feels is necessary.

SOCIALISM - ITALY
SOCIALISM - MANCHESTER

Reconstruction (1939-1951) (may subdiv. geog. except U.S.)   940.53

Also a general directive, but with one exception; United States cannot be added as a subdivision.

RECONSTRUCTION (1939-1951) GREECE

Hotels, motels, etc. (may subdiv. geog. country
or state)   647.728.5

Only the names of countries or states may
be added to this heading.

HOTELS, MOTELS, etc. — FRANCE
HOTELS, MOTELS, etc. — FLORIDA

If the content dealt with lodgings in a city
the heading would read:

LONDON — HOTELS, MOTELS, etc.

Pottery (may subdiv. geog. adjective form, e.g.
Pottery, Chinese, etc.)   666.738

Pottery may be subdivided by any locality as
long as the adjectival form of the name is used.

In other cases, names of places are subdivided by subjects
according to the instructions.

Harbors   386; 387.1; 627

See also Docks; Marinas; Pilots and pilotage;
also names of cities with the subdivision *Harbor*; e.g., Chicago — Harbor, etc.

Further examples of subject divided by place are found under
the names of the models for place: Chicago, Ohio, United
States. Follow these carefully. "Harbor" for example is found
as a subdivision under Chicago, but not under Ohio or United
States.

Chicago — Harbor   386
    xx Harbors

If it were necessary for the subject "harbors" to reflect location by state or country it would be written thus:

HARBORS — CALIFORNIA
HARBORS — NORWAY

Place is a common method of identification and *Sears* provides many examples. Any appropriate term may be subdivided by place even though no model exists. There are no
definite rules to follow in such cases, but keep in mind whether
the subject aspect or the place aspect is most important. Record all decisions in *Sears*.

105

HISTORY   On the library shelf, materials dealing with history are arranged chronologically by country. Subject headings indicating historical periods are also arranged chronologically in the catalog. This is not so in catalogs where the new filing rules are strictly followed. For the present, however, subject headings indicating historical period are found in most catalogs in chronological order as indicated in the subject heading list.

> United States—History—1783-1809   973.4
>   *See also* **Lewis and Clark Expedition (1804-1806);**
>   **Louisiana Purchase; United States—Constitu-**
>   **tional history**
>   *x* Confederation of American colonies
> United States—History—1783-1865   973.5
> United States—History—1801-1805, Tripolitan War
>   973.4
>   *x* Tripoline War
>   *xx* **Pirates**
> United States—History—1812-1815, War of 1812
>   973.5
>   *x* War of 1812
> United States—History—1815-1861   973.5-973.6
>   *See also* **Black Hawk War, 1832**
> United States—1845-1848, War with Mexico   973.6
>   *x* Mexican War, 1845-1848

Figure 8-8

These subject headings must be assigned in the form prescribed. When the time period covered by the item does not coincide with the dates of the subject heading, use the time period that most closely corresponds rather than changing the dates given in *Sears*.

SUMMARY

Classification locates items together on the shelf according to their subjects. Subject headings locate items by subject in the catalog, making it possible to bring out various facets of the subject of a work and to gather common topics under a standard term. To prevent the scattering of related materials, a controlled vocabulary is selected from a standard list. In the United States the two most common lists for general collections are *Sears List of Subject Headings* and *Library of Congress Subject Headings*. Designed on the same general principle, the lists are compatible and may be used together if necessary. General libraries with small collections usually prefer the shorter, simpler, and more general terms found in *Sears*.

A list of subject headings is really a network of subject entries and cross references containing general subjects, specific subjects, divisions of subjects, cross references from subjects not used, references from one subject to related subjects, and notes indicating the scope of a subject. To guide users through this network *see* references (from terms not used to terms used) and *see also* references (from one subject to another, related, one) are suggested in the list. An authority file should be kept to record all decisions about subject headings, and *Sears* leaves the right hand side of each page blank so that terms can be checked as they are used.

The general topic of a work, determined during the technical reading, indicates where to begin to consult the subject list. Scope notes and references aid the selection of headings. The cataloger builds a consistent catalog by using a standard list and following directions carefully.

CHAPTER REVIEW

Terms to understand:

Collections
Word by word filing

Assigning Sears subject headings:

Determine the general subject or subjects by technical reading.
After the classification number has been decided, consult related subject headings in the list.
Select the most specific headings possible, normally limiting the number to three.
Assign the appropriate *see* and *see also* headings.
Record all decisions in *Sears*.

Subject headings — literature:

Do not assign subject headings to single works of literature by one author.
Follow the model provided for literature — "English Literature" with its subdivisions.
For critical works about literature use the subdivision — HISTORY AND CRITICISM.

Geography and history:

Do not subdivide by place without checking the proper subject heading and the models for cities, states, countries.
Observe the chronological arrangement of historical subject headings, fitting the content to the dates in the headings.

107

CHAPTER 9

CATALOGING WITH COPY

THE PROCESS of describing a work, choosing access points, and assigning a classification notation is referred to as ORIGINAL CATALOGING. Many items require original cataloging, including corporate reports, most K-12 textbooks, certain audio-visual materials, and locally printed or produced works. These are examples of the types of materials that the Library of Congress does not place in its collection and does not catalog, therefore prepared copy is rarely available. Cataloging copy is available, however, for most trade books and government documents, and for some AV materials. This copy can be purchased, usually in the form of card sets, from the Library of Congress and publishers and jobbers. Many selection tools, such as the H. W. Wilson *Standard Catalog* series (which includes bibliographies for senior and junior high schools and public libraries as well as fiction and children's collections) give cataloging information. The *Booklist,* a periodical that lists a selection of new material in each issue, prints cataloging information, as does the *Weekly Record,* which lists newly published books weekly.

Some libraries use prepared copy without questioning its accuracy. Others carefully compare this copy with the item in hand and then check with their catalog. At least make sure that the copy matches the work in hand because this cannot be taken for granted. Copy for different editions may differ considerably and sometimes mistakes in ordering occur.

The extent to which catalog copy is checked against the local catalog depends on the policies and working conditions of particular libraries. When many demands are placed on a librarian's time, checking and revising catalog copy may take low priority. If the catalog is considered merely as a finding device for individual items there is little reason to spend time integrating copy in order to standardize access. However, most libraries have open shelves, and patrons search for and retrieve their own materials. They will be most successful when the catalog brings together works of individual authors, when subjects are found together, and when there is some consistency in access points. Only if time is spent checking copy can such a catalog be created.

CATALOGING IN PUBLICATION

The most accessible catalog copy is the CATALOGING IN PUB-
LICATION (CIP) data that is found on the verso (back) of the
title page of most trade books. More than 1800 American publishers now submit books in galley form to the CIP office at
Library of Congress. Materials are cataloged as completely as
possible from their galleys and the information sent to the
publisher, who includes it in the printed book.

CIP Record

```
Library of Congress Cataloging in Publication Data

McCullough, David G.
    Mornings on horseback
    Bibliography; p.
    Includes index


    1. Roosevelt, Theodore, 1858-1919--Childhood
and Youth  2. Presidents--United States--Bio-
graphy  I. Title

E757.M45        973.91'1'0934[B]        81-1697
ISBN 0-671-22711-4
```

Figure 9-1

Because the cataloger sees only the galley proof, which is
unpaged and usually without illustrations, certain areas of description are omitted. These include other title information,

Completed Record: Level Two.

```
McCullough, David G.
    Mornings on horseback / David McCullough.
--New York : Simon and Schuster, c1981.
    445p., [32]p. of plates : ill.
    Bibliography: p. 413 - 424.
    Includes index.


    1. Roosevelt, Theodore, 1858-1919--Childhood
and Youth  2. Presidents--United States--Bio-
graphy  I. Title

                                81-1697
```

Figure 9-2

the statement of responsibility, edition, publication, and physical description areas. When CIP data is used these areas must be added to complete the catalog record.

With the book in hand, it is a simple task for a clerk to complete the cataloging record. Using CIP data is more efficient than doing completely original cataloging. The access points, subject headings, classification number, and notes are all supplied, and the record need not be completed by a professional cataloger. A standard main entry has been selected. However, the information must still be converted into a catalog record, such as a typed or printed card, or micro format.

When relying on CIP data the cataloger first decides which level of description is desired. In Figure 9-2 CIP data is used for Level Two description. Level One description would be formatted as below.

Completed Record: Level One.

```
McCullough, David G.
    Mornings on horseback. -- Simon and Schuster,
1981.
    445p.
    Bibliography : p. 413 - 424.
    Includes index.


    ISBN 0-671-22711-4

    1.  Roosevelt, Theodore, President, U.S.
    2.  Presidents--United States--Biography I. Title
```

Figure 9-3

Completing the description does not complete the cataloging record. Access points and a call number must still be assigned. Since CIP data provides a standard main entry, use as is. If there is a problem of conflict with the catalog, a *see* reference can be used to resolve it. Recommended subject headings and added entries need examination. In Figure 9-1, two Library of Congress subject headings are suggested and subject cards may be prepared for both of them. Some libraries might consider the second heading—PRESIDENTS-UNITED STATES - BIOGRAPHY—too general for retrieval purposes for this particular book and choose not to use it. Other libraries, using *Sears,* might discard both headings and replace with a form selected from *Sears* as illustrated in Figure 9-3. Added entries must be examined with the same care. The CIP data in Figure 9-1 lists only a title added entry, certainly a must for retrieval. Figure 9-4 shows examples of added entries that might be selected for another item. The local library should use only those likely to help the patron find a specific item.

```
History of Wayne County, North Carolina : a collection of histori-
   cal stories created by the Heritage Committee on the Bicenten-
   nial Commission and published in Goldsboro News-argus, April
   6, 1975-July 4, 1976 / Bob Johnson and Charles S. Norwood,
   editors. —Goldsboro,   N.C. : Wayne County Historical Associa-
   tion, 1979.
      x, 239 p., [3] leaves of plates : ill. ; 24 cm.
      Title on spine: Wayne County history.
      "Republished with additions."
      1. Wayne Co., N.C. —History—Addresses, essays, lectures.  2. Wayne Co.,
   N.C. —Biography—Addresses, essays, lectures.   3. Wayne Co., N.C. —
   Genealogy—Addresses, essays, lectures.  I. Johnson, Bob, 1935-  II.
   Norwood, Charles S., 1904-  III. Bicentennial Commission, Goldsboro,
   N.C.  Heritage Committee.   IV. News-argus, Goldsboro, N.C.  V. Wayne
   County Historical Association.   VI. Title: Wayne County history.
   F262.W4H57                    975.6'395                   79-126431
                                    80                          MARC
```

Figure 9-4

In Figure 9-4, the record has been completed with three subject headings and six added entries. In a special collection of Southern history such thorough cataloging might be desirable. In a general collection one subject heading for Wayne Co., N.C. would be adequate, and six added entries for editors, commissions, and a newspaper would be questioned.

Finally, the cataloger must provide a classification number. A library following LCC will normally assign the LCC number as is from CIP. Accepting the DDC number as is may lead to shelving problems.

The Dewey classification number on CIP copy is from the unabridged edition of the DDC in use when the material was cataloged. This may not be the edition of DDC that the library is using. If classification numbers are considered only as location devices this will not matter a great deal, but if the library is attempting to arrange its collection on the shelf in a logical sequence for the browser, the CIP number must be compared against the local shelf list.

Other considerations remain. Various options for arranging material using DDC were discussed in Chapter Seven. Each library makes its own decisions about fiction, biography, critical works, and so forth. If the integrity of the shelving scheme is to be maintained, then the DDC number found on copy must be altered to conform to these local decisions. CIP Dewey numbers seem excessively long. However, prime marks indicate where the numbers can be shortened without destroying the meaning of the notations. A library using the abridged usually finds the shortened number fits into its scheme. However, this isn't true when number building is done. Look at Figure 9-1, the first example of CIP copy. This biography of Theodore Roosevelt can be shelved either in a general biography section [B] or the U.S history number, indicating the biographical form by adding the standard subdivision 0934 from the unabridged to 973.9171'0934. The abridged DDC also has this option. In this case the standard subdivision would be 093 and the completed number 973.91093. A library classifying with the abridged would find it necessary to use the tables from the abridged instead of simply cutting back the CIP number. Finally, as shown in Chapter Seven, the Dewey classification number is completed with the addition of a book or Cutter number.

Because converting the CIP data into the final catalog entry can be a time-consuming project, many libraries prefer to purchase printed cards and use CIP data, if at all, only to create a temporary record in the catalog.

PURCHASED COPY

The Library of Congress sells cards for materials that it catalogs for its own collection. Many high schools, public, and academic libraries purchase them. They are ordered in sets, using the Library of Congress order numbers that are printed on the verso of the title page, in CIP data, in many review sources, and on the LC card itself in the lower left-hand corner. The cards arrive without subject headings, added entries, and call numbers, which are typed in at the local library. Do not alter the body of the card (the description) which is normally Level Two. Otherwise, apply the same procedures to adapting LC cards for the collection as are used for CIP data. If some added entries or subject headings are to be omitted, simply cross them out of the tracings. If it is necessary to add an access point or change subject headings, be sure to record the decision in the tracings. Suggested call numbers are printed at the bottom of LC cards, but the library can assign any call number.

Many copy sources also indicate whether or not the cataloging copy is available in machine readable form; LC cataloging

```
Hitchcock, Anthony, 1940-
     Country inns, lodges and historic hotels of
the Middle Atlantic States / by Anthony Hitchcock and
Jean Lindgren. -- New York : B. Franklin, c1979.
     190p. : ill. ; 17 cm. -- (The Compleat travel-
er's companion)
     Includes index

     ISBN 0-89102-182-5: $6.95.  ISBN 0-8910-157-4
(pbk): $3.95
     1. Hotels, taverns, etc.--Middle States-
Directories  I. Lindgren, Jean, 1941.  joint
author  II. Title  III. Series

TX907.H539          647'.9474          79-10982
                                          MARC
```

Figure 9-5

information can also be purchased in this way. In the mid-
1960s, the Library of Congress began distributing machine
readable cataloging (MARC). Sixteen selected libraries first
received these tapes containing the bibliographic records of
books cataloged at the Library of Congress. Those libraries
tested and experimented with the MARC format, which was
soon greatly expanded and revised. In 1969 the MARC Distribution Service began. For an annual fee the subscriber receives each week a magnetic tape containing cataloging done
at the Library during the previous week.

Development of the MARC format led to the establishment
of BIBLIOGRAPHIC UTILITIES, computer data bases of bibliographic records. The largest of these, OCLC, contains more
than 8 million records and provides, via computer terminals,
cataloging information to a number of institutions. These
member institutions in turn contribute their own unique records to the data base.

MARC subscribers have always numbered approximately
one hundred, but many more libraries have benefited from
the MARC tapes. Jobbers, the bibliographic utilities, and
other suppliers of cataloging data subscribe to MARC and
provide thousands of libraries with standard cataloging copy
from them. When an item is also on MARC, this is indicated
in the lower right hand corner of the LC card, directly below
the order number.

Publishers and jobbers often supply cards with a simplified format for the lower grades and for children's collections. Check subject headings, recommended call numbers,
and added entries. Notes may be added to cataloging at any

113

descriptive level. If necessary, add additional information (such as grade level) in a note.

Whatever the source of printed copy, the catalog is a more useful tool if access points, subject headings, and classification are integrated into the catalog, thus gathering together the works of one author, the editions of one work, and material dealing with the same or similar subjects.

CATALOGING PROFILES

It is possible under certain circumstances to order copy that is designed for the use of a particular library. OCLC assists its customers, or regional vendors, in developing a CATALOGING PROFILE, or format, by which all of its copy is prepared. Thus a library can choose to omit notes, LC numbers, or any other area from the final product. Jobbers also provide certain amount of customized service. The following is an example of a jobber's specification sheet with both standard and alternate specifications.

CATALOGING SPECIFICATIONS

Please check the standard or alternate specification you desire for each of the categories listed below. Where you specify an alternate, it will be supplied without additional charge.

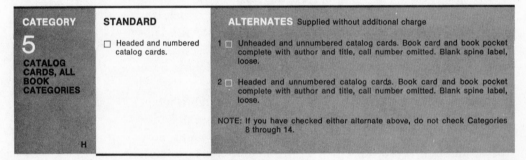

CATEGORY	STANDARD	ALTERNATES Supplied without additional charge
5 CATALOG CARDS, ALL BOOK CATEGORIES H	☐ Headed and numbered catalog cards.	1 ☐ Unheaded and unnumbered catalog cards. Book card and book pocket complete with author and title, call number omitted. Blank spine label, loose. 2 ☐ Headed and unnumbered catalog cards. Book card and book pocket complete with author and title, call number omitted. Blank spine label, loose. NOTE: If you have checked either alternate above, do not check Categories 8 through 14.

This jobber, as a standard service, supplies catalog cards with printed headings (subject headings and added entries) and call numbers. However, on the right are listed those options available to libraries that wish to supply their own headings and/or call numbers.

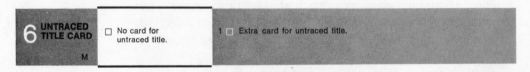

6 UNTRACED TITLE CARD M	☐ No card for untraced title.	1 ☐ Extra card for untraced title.

Some items, especially textbooks, may have titles that are considered non-distinctive, for example *Arithmetic, Basic Chemistry, Spanish One.* Many libraries do not trace, that is, do not create an entry for such titles, reasoning that they are practically useless for retrieval purposes. Collections that house few texts, or contain only texts, and institutions that divide their catalogs, might find title entry useful.

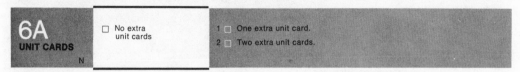

A unit set will contain a card for every entry, and a main entry card for the shelf list. Some libraries may want to create additional entries, and may keep other files. One or two extra unit cards would therefore be necessary.

Public libraries often have one catalog for their entire collection. In order to aid their users in selecting materials, those items intended for children and young people are identified with a "J" in front of the call number. Such a designation makes little sense in a library or media center whose entire collection is intended for juveniles.

There are options, as discussed in Chapter Seven, for the classification of both fiction and biographies, and these are illustrated by the number of choices offered for the call numbers in those areas. Some allow the library to add its own Cutter number; others supply letters for the author or biographical surname. A Dewey number is available if the Library of Congress has assigned one and recorded it on MARC tape.

11 INDIVIDUAL BIOGRAPHY (D)

Standard	Alternates	
☐ B with biographee's surname.	1 ☐ B with first three letters of biographee's surname.	9 ☐ 92.
	2 ☐ B with first two letters of biographee's surname.	A ☐ 921 with biographee's surname.
	3 ☐ B with first letter of biographee's surname.	B ☐ 921 with first three letters of biographee's surname.
	4 ☐ B.	C ☐ 921 with first two letters of biographee's surname.
	5 ☐ 92 with biographee's surname.	D ☐ 921 with first letter of biographee's surname.
	6 ☐ 92 with first three letters of biographee's surname.	E ☐ 921.
	7 ☐ 92 with first two letters of biographee's surname.	F ☐ No call number.
	8 ☐ 92 with first letter of biographee's surname.	

12 COLLECTIVE BIOGRAPHY (E)

Standard	Alternates	
☐ 920 with first letter of author's surname.	1 ☐ 920 with first two letters of author's surname.	5 ☐ 92 with first two letters of author's surname.
	2 ☐ 920 with first three letters of author's surname.	6 ☐ 92 with first three letters of author's surname.
	3 ☐ 920.	7 ☐ 92.
	4 ☐ 92 with first letter of author's surname.	8 ☐ No call number.

School and public libraries often indicate EASY BOOKS (mainly picture books intended primarily for young children) with an E rather than a classification number, or an F to provide a special collection for young users. All E books will then be filed together, perhaps by author, perhaps in no particular order. Some libraries may prefer to shelve easy books with the rest of the collection and can order Dewey numbers if they have been assigned.

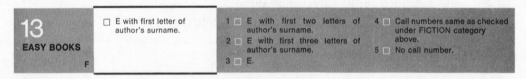

13 EASY BOOKS (F)

Standard	Alternates	
☐ E with first letter of author's surname.	1 ☐ E with first two letters of author's surname.	4 ☐ Call numbers same as checked under FICTION category above.
	2 ☐ E with first three letters of author's surname.	5 ☐ No call number.
	3 ☐ E.	

If the call number is regarded strictly as a finding device a library will accept a Dewey number as given, with or without letters of the author's surname, depending on whether a Cutter number is used. Otherwise the option of no call number is selected.

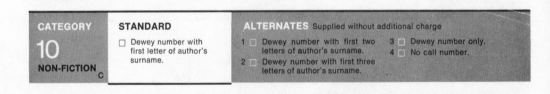

CATEGORY 10 NON-FICTION (C)

STANDARD	ALTERNATES Supplied without additional charge	
☐ Dewey number with first letter of author's surname.	1 ☐ Dewey number with first two letters of author's surname.	3 ☐ Dewey number only.
	2 ☐ Dewey number with first three letters of author's surname.	4 ☐ No call number.

These are examples of specifications developed for a small public or school library with a fairly general collection. An academic library, or a library with a large collection, would be offered others (for example, LC numbers instead of Dewey).

SUMMARY

Cataloging copy can be found in any number of sources including the CIP data in most trade books, bibliographies that are used to select materials, and cards that are prepared by publishers, producers, or jobbers. The busy librarian may be tempted to use this copy as is, although it may not be entirely accurate for the item in hand. Editions can vary for books of the same title from the same publisher; perhaps only portions of an extensive multi-media kit have been purchased, or portions of an item may simply be missing. Similar problems arise when libraries use cataloging copy from a bibliographic utility. Copy retrieved must still match the item in hand. When users select materials from the catalog, any details that affect their use should certainly be edited.

When description matches the item in hand, it should be used as is. However, it may be necessary to modify other parts of copy, whether CIP or prepared cards. Certain access points may be unnecessary in a particular collection, or, more rarely, additional access points should be added.

If a library strives to shelve like materials together, then Dewey numbers may need modification from those suggested. If cataloging is purchased from a jobber or a vendor, it is often possible to plan a cataloging profile that meets the needs of a particular institution. Whether cataloging is retrieved from CIP, a data base, a publisher, or an LC card, editing the copy produces more accurate records.

CHAPTER REVIEW

Terms to remember:

bibliographic utilities
Cataloging In Publication (CIP)
cataloging profile
easy books
original cataloging

Finding cataloging copy:

In selection sources such as *Standard Catalog,* or a bibliographic
   tool such as *Weekly Record.*
On verso of title page (CIP).
Purchased cards from LC.
MARC tapes from LC.
Cards from jobbers and publishers.
Cataloging data from bibliographic utilities.

Using catalog copy:

Match to item in hand.
Use description as is when matched.
Check DDC number so like subjects will be placed together.
Mark out unwanted access points.

CHAPTER **10**

KEEPING THE RECORDS

SINCE LIBRARIANS are spending the money of others, accurate record keeping and accounting is necessary, but the amount varies from system to system. For example, a librarian in a small branch library may find that a number of records are handled by the central office. On the other hand, some small libraries may keep as many records as a large institution without having the same number of support staff. Whatever the number of staff or the system used, the purpose of each record should be examined and none should be kept that is not absolutely necessary, or required by law.

TRACKING MATERIALS

A nation attempts to keep track of its citizens with records, with birth and death certificates, and with individual designators such as social security numbers. In much the same manner librarians keep control of materials in the collection. In order to keep records accurately each item is first assigned a designator, commonly an accession number. Every item acquired is stamped with a number. This number is recorded in the shelf list and circulation records. An automatic stamping machine makes this a simple task. The numbers may run in a continuing sequence, starting with a number one for the first item acquired, and so on; or a break can be made by incorporating the year into the number. Thus the first work received in 1982 would be given the number 82-0001; the second, 82-0002, proceeding through the year. Accession numbers thus provide a running account of numbers of materials acquired. Some libraries assign each format a different series of accession numbers, but this is confusing, almost impossible with the proliferation of formats, and not recommended.

Accession numbers are not always used. When, in such circumstances, DUPLICATES of an item are acquired, it is necessary to mark both the shelf list and the items with a copy number. Because duplicate items may be acquired after long intervals, or may be replacements, it is difficult to keep accurate records in this way. This practice does not supply items

Accession Number, Shelf List Cards

119

with a unique number, and it is therefore not recommended. Another way of providing a unique number is to use either the ISBN or the LC card order number, both of which are recorded on most cataloging copy. Although publishers and jobbers use these standard numbers to keep track of their stock, libraries have been slow to realize their usefulness. These numbers can, however, serve in the record keeping process and are retrieval points in most automated bibliographic systems. Either can serve as an appropriate unique designator, but the LC card order number with its year and five digits (83-33421) is not quite so unwieldy as the ISBN.

To assist in keeping an inventory, individual accession numbers are recorded on the shelf list card, thus providing a record of every item in the collection, not just every title as the catalog does. Although the catalog does not normally reveal how many copies of an individual title are owned, the shelf list does supply this information. When an item is withdrawn from the collection, the accession number is deleted. Instead of one shelf list card for one title with all accession numbers, a separate shelf list card can be provided for each item. This makes adding and deleting duplicates a simpler process because it does not involve pulling the shelf list card and erasing or typing in a number each time a copy is removed or added.

Accession numbers that have been retired should never be reused. If the item has been lost or stolen it may well reappear. Reuse of numbers also removes any value the accession number may have for statistical purposes.

Other information recorded on the shelf list card depends on library policy. Some libraries record price in order to charge clients who lose items. Libraries that routinely charge the latest price in *Books in Print*, or charge a uniform fee according to each category of material, need not record it.

Circulation
All libraries that lend materials must keep records, but some libraries need to know more than others. For example, a large public library may want to know who has an item only when the item becomes overdue, whereas most academic libraries want to be able to locate materials at any time. Computer circulation systems are now a familiar sight in both large and small libraries, and microcomputer circulation programs are readily available. Before any circulation system is developed, whether manual or automated, a library should think carefully about what circulation information is necessary for its operation; for instance, is it necessary to know what each borrower has currently? It probably is in any system such as a

school, college, or business library, where the status of those entitled to use the collection may change suddenly. School librarians could face the prospect of searching through several thousand cards to find out if a withdrawing student has outstanding materials. Filing behind a user I.D. number provides such information, but makes it more difficult to keep up with overdue materials.

Is it necessary to know where each individual item is from the moment it is checked out? Again it depends. Academic, school, or special libraries often have a policy of calling in material when others have need of it. These libraries make an effort to keep such a record for each item. Public libraries, however, will not usually notify a user to bring in materials unless they are overdue, and are usually only interested in knowing about an item when it is not returned on time.

What circulation records to keep should depend on what a library needs to know. This is equally true for all library records. When computers are used to do many of these tasks it is imperative that the library be able to define their functions clearly and logically.

Most readers identify serials with PERIODICALS, but these **Serials** can also include newspapers, yearbooks, proceedings, bulletins—in fact, any publication issued in parts, and intended to be continued indefinitely. Many people who would never think of reading a book depend on periodicals for information, and serials are an important part of library collections. Although the general principles for cataloging books also apply to these materials, there are several differences, and many libraries do not include them in the catalog. But whether cataloged or not, serial records must be kept, and their very nature can create some problems. For most library items, once they are ordered, processed, and shelved, the record keeping is complete until the item is withdrawn. Not so with serials, especially periodicals. Because they are issued in parts, record keeping is a continuing process. Libraries regard it as a serious business when periodicals are missing from the collection, for they are expensive to order both in terms of money and time, and they are popular items. It is reasonable, therefore, to spend some time and thought on developing an efficient system of serials control.

Users want to know which serial titles are in a library, and whether any issues are missing. Librarians also want to be sure that they are getting what they paid for, and that the last issue due has arrived. Records must be kept to answer these questions.

Serial orders are placed in different ways. For example, many systems annually place orders with jobbers, and normally all a librarian does is indicate titles to be added or deleted. If a library receives only a very few titles, however, orders are probably placed with individual publishers. No matter how they are ordered, all serials, periodicals, and newspapers should be checked in on arrival. If this is not done efficiently, titles are lost, users are frustrated, and the library wastes money.

Periodicals and newspapers are checked in by title. Check-in cards can be purchased for different types of serials. These cards provide places to record the name of the publication and to check each issue in by date. The check-in card should be typed at the same time the order is placed so there is no confusion about the title. This check-in card can also serve as the record for the user, and be stored as a page in a notebook, in a card file, in a VISIBLE FILE, or on a computer tape. Besides title and issues received, other information can also be recorded, such as purchasing source, binding information, etc. Serials constantly change titles. When that occurs simply start a new record and place a note to that effect on the old one. When periodicals and newspapers do not appear it is necessary to notify the publisher or jobber as soon as possible to assure service. This process is called CLAIMING. Some systems will claim all periodicals centrally; in others each library is responsible. Claims that are not filed promptly may not be honored by publishers.

RE-CATALOGING, RE-CLASSIFICATION, AND WITHDRAWALS

Decisions involved in re-cataloging and re-classifying have been discussed elsewhere. Whatever the philosophical approach to this problem, a certain amount will always be necessary, and this requires a careful change of each record. Besides such changes as are made on the item itself, the shelf list record, each catalog record, and any other record that has this information must be changed. If this is not done accurately and completely there will be such confusion about the item that it would have been better to have made no change at all. Large libraries have defined programs for re-classification and often have a paraprofessional staff to assist. In a small institution, this is another task to be fitted into the daily workload. No matter what the situation, there should be a written procedure to prevent mishap. The same procedures are followed when an item is withdrawn, this time, however, the record is not changed, but removed. Some librarians leave records in the catalog long after an item has disappeared in the expectation that it will someday return. This is really not fair to the user, who may spend a great deal of time searching for a work that is no longer available.

INVENTORY

Businesses take regular stock of their inventory, and libraries may follow suit. Some libraries take this rite so seriously they close the collection to the public annually and track down every leaflet. Others never take formal inventory but manage equally well. The process of inventory-taking is not difficult. The materials on the shelves are simply compared to the shelf list. First any special collections that contain items that have been removed from their classified position are broken up and reshelved in their proper shelf list order. Preferably, teams of two should do the work, one checking the shelf list as the other reads the shelf. Any card with unchecked numbers is turned on end, and any item found incorrectly marked is pulled, to be corrected later. When the shelf list is checked against all the materials being circulated, the inventory is complete and those shelf list cards that show missing material removed. A record is made of missing items and some time later decisions can be made about replacement or withdrawal.

Inventories are expensive activities in terms of time spent, and there is little rationale for their routine occurrence. If shelves are read frequently and accurately and indications are that losses are few, inventories could be rare. Instead of taking a thorough inventory, in which time is wasted counting items that rarely circulate, some libraries spot-check popular areas to get an indication of loss. If accurate records of additions and replacements are kept, it should not be necessary to be taking inventory constantly to arrive at a more or less correct count of items. After all, inventories can become incorrect seconds after they are completed. There is an old library saying, "If you don't miss it, you didn't need it," which contains a lot of truth. For those items that have never been missed, that no patron has ever inquired about, or conversely, that have never left the shelf, money and time spent on inventory are wasted.

There are times when it is necessary to inventory. When a collection is to be broken up, or moved to a new location, it makes sense to inventory. If, because of losses, some kind of detection system is put in place, inventory should be taken before and after the system is installed. A change in format of catalog, from card to COM cat, for example, would surely create a need for an inventory. But normally, lack of access by users, and amount of time spent by staff, cannot be justified for routine inventories.

STATISTICS

Statistical information may be divided into two types; that which shows the amount of work done, and that which records the holdings of the library. Statistics should be kept only to the extent that they supply useful information, such as those titles in each format, and sometimes in each category, that have been added or subtracted. Circulation figures are sometimes regarded as an indication of work done, and many libraries are legally required to report circulation figures although they have little to do with services provided. It is difficult to judge which statistics are useful and which are not. Many libraries routinely report on numbers of new titles added, but even that number means little unless it is interpreted. For instance, how does that figure compare with acquisitions of libraries of similar size, with that of a year ago, a decade ago, and what do these comparisons signify?

When records are kept by computer, statistics are more easily generated than when all counting is done manually. When a circulation and reserve system is automated, for example, it is possible to keep records not only of how many times an item circulated, but also of how many times that item was requested and unavailable — an even more useful statistic for selection purposes. A librarian with little time to keep statistics, and even less time to interpret them, keeps statistical reports to a minimum and compiles them only when they serve a useful purpose.

SUMMARY

A certain amount of record keeping is necessary in any library. Policy and commonsense should dictate how much. At a minimum, records are normally kept of the number of items added or withdrawn, and the number of items classified in various subject areas. Circulation generates more records, for libraries must know who has their materials and when they are due. Inaccurate record keeping can be expensive when serials, especially periodicals, are carelessly controlled and unreceived copies are not noted. Unless there is a good reason to spend time and money making an inventory of a collection, it should not be done routinely. Even small libraries can use microcomputers to record statistics, and librarians need to analyze and justify their present practices in light of new technology.

CHAPTER REVIEW

Terms to remember:

claiming
duplicates
periodicals
serials
visible file

The shelf list record:

Records each item, whether a duplicate title or not.
Provides an inventory of the collection.
Must be kept current.

Circulation records:

Record materials that are lent to users.
Are designed according to a library's need for information:
    for example, some libraries are interested only in overdue
    circulation records.

Serials records:

Must be kept current. Users must know titles and dates in
    collections. Librarians must make sure issues arrive.

Inventory records and statistics:

Should be kept only when they supply useful information for
    decision making, or when required by law.

CHAPTER 11

BEHIND THE WORKROOM DOOR

THE NUMBER of typing, filing and processing chores that must be done at the local library has greatly decreased in the last decade. Cooperative and commercial processing centers are now so well established that even the smallest library can routinely order materials cataloged, ready to be shelved. In many libraries a computer has taken over certain routine tasks such as keeping records and filing entries. But there are always some chores that only the individual library can do for itself and these will vary from institution to institution.

A special library that collects only in-house materials such as reports, bulletins, and newsletters will probably be responsible for complete local processing and cataloging. Gifts are often handled by individual libraries, as are certain audiovisual formats. Local records must be maintained for serials. Commercial services do not provide analytic cards or references, nor do they help maintain a catalog. Many of these tasks may be done by clerks and volunteers, but the librarian should develop simple and effective procedures for guiding their work. If date due slips fall out before items can be returned, if spine labels slide off before shelving, if catalog cards are rarely or improperly filed, a library cannot run efficiently. No matter what the level of automation or centralization no library can lock the workroom door permanently.

MECHANICAL PREPARATION AND MAINTENANCE

For those materials that are to be circulated manually, pocket and card must be typed with the item's identification.

Type the call number in the upper left hand corner of the card and of the pocket. Add the accession or copy number on the right. Type the author's last name and title proper. The card is filed while the item is in circulation, and quickly identified by the information on the pocket when it is returned.

Pockets are uniformly pasted according to library practice in either the front or the back of the item. Only those items that circulate require a pocket and card, but all items must be stamped with ownership identification. Material should be

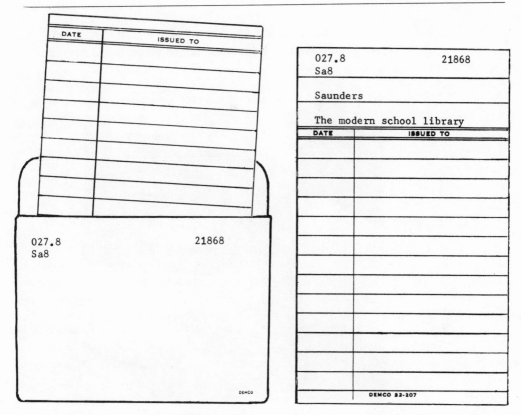

Figure 11-1

stamped both internally and externally in uniform positions. Label the call number on the spine, using self-adhesive labels. If plastic book jackets are used, place label on jackets.

NON-BOOK
MATERIALS

When non-book materials first appeared in library collections there was great confusion about the best way to process and circulate them. Professional meetings were often taken up by discussions of how to shelve cassettes and stamp fiche. These matters have virtually ceased to be professional concerns. Publishers and distributors now package many formats so they are easily intershelved with books. Library supply houses offer storage and display units, as well as processing materials, for a variety of items, including cassette tapes and video disks. However, the sudden appearance of a new format to be housed, cataloged, and circulated will usually present some unique problems.

Although computer-assisted instruction and other interactive computer programs have been in use for some time, computer software was rarely found in libraries or school media centers. The advent of microcomputers has changed this. Microcomputers are programmed by small record-like, paper

127

encased disks, called FLOPPY DISKS, which can store a variety of educational, informational, or recreational programs.

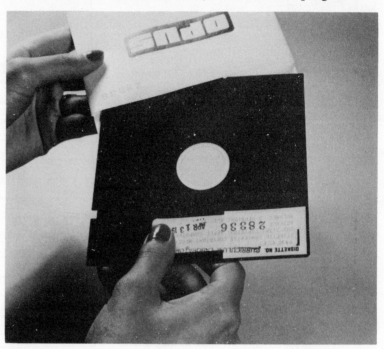

Figure 11-2

These disks have rapidly found their way into library collections and supply catalogs sell a variety of storage units for them. Floppy disks can be stored in rotary disk organizers, in three-ring binders, in plastic modules, in pocket folders, or in hanging files. However filed, each disk remains in its paper cover and should be touched only when enclosed by this envelope. Identification labels are fixed to the upper-left-hand corner. The envelope itself may be marked with a soft-tipped marker.

Because many forms of non-book media, including floppy disks, can be copied easily in the library, it has become a great temptation to maintain "back-up copies" of such material. Institutions that would never dream of duplicating *Guinness Book of Records* because it is so often lost or stolen will argue that the potential for damage makes the copying of each software title a necessity for collection maintenance. This is encouraged by the fact that the law does allow some copying, although only for archival purposes. If everyone were to build a collection of copied media soon no publisher would find it worthwhile to produce high-quality programs. Publishers are already reluctant to send easily pirated materials for preview. When immediate access is vital, or when necessary data could be lost, a replacement copy should be maintained. Either make a workable backup copy, or buy two copies. Before routinely producing backup copies for all media, consider the expense involved in creating copies that may never be needed, and remember that a copy is never the original. Data can be lost on a copied disk, colors fade from video duplicates, and sound deteriorates when reproduced.

A COM Cat, or on-line catalog, does not require maintenance in the same way the card catalog does. Card catalogs require filing time, cards must be shifted as drawers fill, guide cards and outside labels must be provided, and individual cards pulled as items are removed from the collection. Each drawer should never be more than three-quarters full. Shift cards when necessary so that drawers do not become too tightly packed. Include guides that break up the alphabet for the convenience of users.

Card Catalog Maintenance

Even those libraries that rely on purchased copy or central processing services find that they acquire some materials for which catalog cards must be typed. These typewritten cards should be made to the same specifications as the printed ones.

Typing Cards

When possible, catalog at level one. There are three indentions on a typed card. Normally the FIRST INDENTION is nine spaces from the left edge, the SECOND INDENTION is twelve spaces, and the THIRD INDENTION is fourteen spaces.

Skeleton Card Showing Indentions

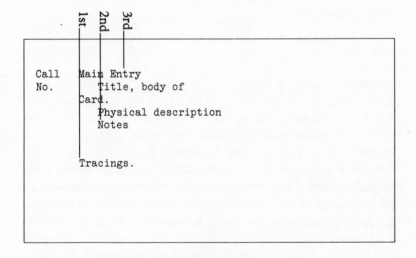

```
      1st  2nd  3rd

Call    Main Entry
No.         Title, body of
        Card.
            Physical description
            Notes


        Tracings.
```

Figure 11-3

The call number is typed one full space in from the left edge of the card on the third line down from the top. The main entry begins on the third line at first indention. If the main entry is longer than one line, the second line begins at third indention.

When main entry is under title, the entire body of the card follows at second indention. This spacing, discussed in Chapter Two, is known as hanging indention.

When main entry is under personal name or corporate body, the title is typed on the line below at second indention. The body of the card follows after the title, with the next lines brought back to the first indention, making a paragraph form. Remember each element is separated by a full stop.

Physical description follows the body of the card and begins at second indention. Notes follow one full line below, beginning at the second indention. If longer than one full line, continue at first indention.

Tracings are typed at least three lines below the catalog information at first indention. When there is no room on the face of the card, tracings may be typed on the back. Subject headings and added entries above the main entry begin at second indention on the second line of typing. If they are too long for one line, the second line begins at third indention.

Each library draws up its own typing manual, and there are probably no two libraries that follow exactly the same rules. Unless starting a new collection, study established cataloging rules. Unfortunately, in some libraries, no rules seem to have been established at all. In such a case, follow the above guidelines, and produce typed cards as uniformly and as neatly as possible. Additional typing guides will be found in the appendix.

PREPARING ANALYTICS

Users of large, diverse, library collections seldom go away empty-handed. A small collection serves many demands, but has fewer items to satisfy them. In an effort to serve more users with fewer materials, some catalogers make ANALYTIC ENTRIES, that is entries that provide access to parts of works. Analytics are most often prepared for collective works such as anthologies. Analytic cards cannot be purchased and must be prepared in the individual libraries, according to their needs. The following are examples of their use.

Subject Analytics

There are books, films, and filmstrips concerned with caring for almost any pet that can be acquired, and some libraries may own a variety of these. Others may own only a few general items about pets. In order that these general materials can serve those users searching for only "hamsters" or "mice" in addition to the subject heading "pets," analytic subject entries are made for the individual pets included.

Collective biographies are usually given a general heading, such as ARTISTS, FRENCH. In a small collection, a subject analytic card can be made for each individual artist discussed.

Students may be assigned individual plays to read and come to the library for them. The library may purchase plays only in collections, as the cost per play is less. Since the students may look under either the author or the title of the desired play, entries will be made under the author-title, and in reverse under the title-author. These will be typed as headings, above the main entry.

Author-Title: Title-Author Analytics

Sherwood, Robert   ) Author and
    The petrified forest) title analytic

    The petrified forest) Title and author
Sherwood, Robert   ) analytic

For a collection of works by one author, title analytics can be made for each individual work. The author's name is the main entry.

      Romeo and Juliet
   Shakespeare, William
    Shakespeare's tragedies

There are reference books and indexes such as *Essay and General Literature Index, Biography Index,* short story and play indexes, that analyze the contents of many printed collections. These can be considered extensions of the catalog and should be used as much as possible rather than typing analytic cards. Shelve these near the catalog and instruct library patrons in their use. Often, however, a small budget makes it difficult to purchase these tools. In addition, indexes do not contain very recent publications.

At best, however, these indexes will provide access to collections in books. For collections of titles in sound recording, computer programs, filmstrips and other media, there are no such guides. Sometimes only a single analytic card is necessary. For example, in a school library, a certain poem might be in demand each year, and a single analytic would save everyone a lot of time. Public libraries often do analytics for certain holiday materials that are requested every season.

131

Typing Analytics
and Cross References

Ideally, analytics are simply added to a unit card by typing the additional information above the main entry at second indention. Two-line author and title analytics are typed two lines above the main entry at the second and third indention. Title and author entries are made at third and second. If all of the card must be typed, use a truncated form, giving only call number, main entry, title, publisher, and date.

When cross reference cards are used in the catalog to refer users either from terms and names not used (*see* references), or to related terms that might be useful (*see also*), they must also be typed. Type the term not used three lines from the top of the card at the second indention. Two lines below, and at the third indention, type *see*. Two lines below this, and at the first indention, type the term used.

```
          Oxford Book of American Verse

             see

          The New Oxford Book of American
          Verse
```

Follow exactly the same format for *see also* references. Type all subjects in capital letters.

```
             FAMILY

                see also

          CLANS AND CLAN SYSTEM
          HOME
          PARENT AND CHILD
             see also names of members of the
                family, e.g., CHILDREN; FATHERS; ETC.
```

Creasey wrote under many names, and some libraries will pull these forms together for the user. *See also* cards can either

```
          Creasey, John

             see also

          Ashe, Gordon
          Halliday, Michael
          Hunt, Kyle
          Marric, J. J.
          Morton, Anthony
          York, Jeremy
```

be filed following, or in front of, entries of the same word, phrase, or name.

FILING

Whether they are duplicates, original cataloging, or analytics, entries, to be useful, must be filed into the catalog. The tool for filing is *ALA Filing Rules*. Filing can be confusing in a large dictionary catalog. The confusion is lessened when the catalog is divided into one section for author/title, and another for subject, because subject entries are usually not filed in strict alphabetical order, but according to special rules.

All catalogs are filed either word by word, or letter by letter. Most users are unaware of the distinction, yet it can make a considerable difference to the order in which entries are found.

Word by Word	*Letter by Letter*
San Diego	Sanchez, George Isadore
San Domingo	Sand, George
San Francisco	Sandburg, Carl
Sanchez, George Isadore	San Diego
Sand, George	San Domingo
Sandburg, Carl	Sande, Earl
Sande, Earl	San Francisco

When filing word by word, the rule is "nothing before something." With word-by-word filing, San Francisco is filed before Sanchez because of the space (nothing) after San. Letter-by-letter filing ignores spaces. Most card catalogs are filed word by word, whereas many reference sources file letter by letter.

Word-by-word filing is recommended in the new rules, and the rule "nothing before something" remains. The basic principle of the new rules is to "file as is," although previous filing practice stressed filing "as if." For example, Dr. was filed as if it were written Doctor, Mr. as if it were Mister, and the numeral 4 as if it were written four. In the 1980 rules numerals are filed before letters, roman numerals are treated as if they were arabic, and written numbers are filed alphabetically. Words that can be spelled in different ways (i.e., honour or honor), and abbreviations, are filed exactly as written. If followed completely, new filing practice means subject headings will also be filed as is and many former practices will disappear. The rules recommend liberal use of information cards and *see* and *see also* references to guide users.

Filing "as is" will in the long run make a difficult task simpler for both filer and user. However, it will not solve every filing problem. Considering that an entry misfiled is an item lost, it is good practice to study the structure of any catalog before attempting to file, and to have a copy of the rules to help with such problems as filing Teofile de la Toore, Jose de la Torre Bueno and DeKalb, Illinois. For accuracy, file twice, once above the rod, and make a second check before dropping the cards.

SPECIAL PROBLEMS: SERIALS, MAPS, KITS, AND ELECTRONIC SOFTWARE

Serials   Serials can be issued in any format and include annuals, yearbooks, newspapers, and periodicals. Because they are issued in successive parts and continue for some time, their acquisition involves a certain amount of record keeping (see Chapter 10). Serial records, especially those for periodicals, are often kept separate but follow regular rules if they are entered in the main catalog. Identify the Chief Source of Information (Figure 4-2) and enter under either title or author. For serials, indicate on the catalog record not only what titles are available, but which issues or parts are owned by the library. Record this information in the NUMERIC area, immediately after the edition statement. This area is unique to serials. Edition information and statements of responsibility areas are infrequently given for periodicals, and the numeric area is usually recorded directly after the title. Record the designation of the first issue in the library collection.

If the first issue is also identified by a date, give the numbering before the date.

> Online — vol 1, no 1 (Jan. 1977) -

Since at this point there is no way of knowing how long the serial will either be issued or received by the library, the entry is left "open," indicated by the dash. This OPEN ENTRY is closed when the last issue arrives.

> Online — vol 1, no 1 (Jan. 1977) -
> vol. 4, no 12 (Dec. 1980)

Serials frequently change titles. When this occurs supply a reference card to tie the titles together, and begin cataloging under the new title.

Some serials, such as annuals and yearbooks (*Yearbook of Agriculture*) are issued with individual titles and deal with a variety of topics. Libraries may catalog these as serials, but it is usually more practicable to separate, catalog, and classify them as single works.

Serials in periodical form are important reference sources and are often stored as a permanent part of the collection instead of being discarded. Titles may be bound into volumes and shelved in a special section, or on the regular shelves according to their classification number. To save space, many libraries prefer to subscribe to a microform edition which they keep in a permanent file, allowing the regular edition to be circulated and eventually discarded.

Maps come in many forms: small sheets, large sheets, folders, wall maps, and globes. Many libraries do not catalog maps, but add them to a vertical file, arranged by geographical area. Larger or more important maps may be cataloged according to normal rules using the Chief Source of Information (Figure 4-2). The scale of a map should be recorded in the MATHEMATICAL DATA AREA, located immediately after the edition area. Use this area only in cartographic materials, and if the scale is not easily determined, omit this detail.

Maps

> Proceed with the word "scale"

> Scale 1 inch to the mile or
>   1: 160,000

When several maps are cataloged as a unit simply indicate:

Scales vary

Kits   Kits, or multimedia, contain two or more categories of materials packaged as a unit with a unit title. Normally the components are intended to be used together and no format is considered predominant. When this is the case use the container title as the collective title for the item. List the formats making up the kit in the physical description area, adding no further description.

```
Radlauer, Ed
    Drag racing [kit] / written and photographed
by Ed Radlauer -- Glendale, Calif. : Bowman,
1971.
    1 sound disc, 5 booklets, 1 filmstrip,
1 teacher guide
```

If a complete physical description of every item is necessary, give each a separate line.

Sometimes, however, cataloging entire kits leads to trouble at the circulation desk. Perhaps the user wants only part of a kit, or the size makes it difficult to manage. Kits may be separated and the sections processed, cataloged, and circulated as separate items. For example, a school owns a cassette filmstrip series on the five Scandinavian countries entitled *Northwest Europe*. This kit can logically be broken into five items, with the cataloger supplying the titles Norway, Sweden, etc. Formats can also be cataloged separately. If this kit arrived with study posters, these could be separated and cataloged using the GMD [picture]. These are practical decisions to be made by each library.

Electronic   AACR2 defines a machine-readable data file as "a body of
Software   information coded by methods that require the use of a machine (typically a computer) for processing"; and provides

a general materials designator [machine-readable data file] for such materials (Figure 4-1). The descriptive rules make no reference to the familiar microcomputer floppy disk and may seem complicated to those without some knowledge of computers. The following suggestions are for catalogers in public and school libraries who are buying commercially produced programs to inform or entertain and who wish to integrate these into an omni catalog following standard rules, and for those users who are not familiar with computers.

A program's internal use label (a machine-readable identifier) is comparable to a book's title page. If no such label exists, catalog from any documentation available. If possible, describe at level one.

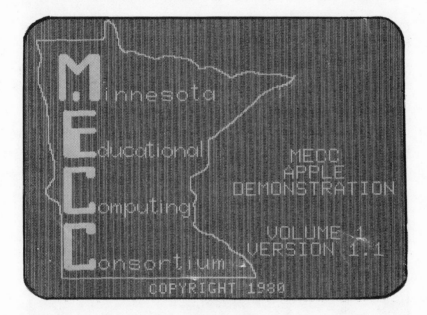

Figure 11-4

The above, a machine-readable identifier for a floppy disk, is the Chief Source of Information.

The Minnesota Educational Computing Consortium writes and distributes educational software, and is usually referred to in the literature as MECC. This work does not appear to fit into those categories entered under corporate name, so title entry would be appropriate. Because some users will search for all materials from MECC, an added entry should be provided to bring them together. A *see* cross reference card would refer users from Minnesota Educational Computing

```
371.33   MECC Apple demonstration [machine-readable data
MEC          file] / Minnesota Educational Computing
             Consortium -- St. Paul : MECC, 1980.
             1 floppy disk (1 vol. version 1.1) + guide

             Use with Apple II microcomputer




             1.  Teaching materials  I. MECC
        II.  Title: Apple demonstration
```

Consortium to MECC. This is a case in which additional title access could be useful, especially if most titles of this material are introduced with MECC.

The term "floppy disk" is commonly used in the literature, so it is selected as the specific material designator.

Level one cataloging does not restrict the note areas. Because disks do not run on all machines the user must be told the correct machine for the program in the notes.

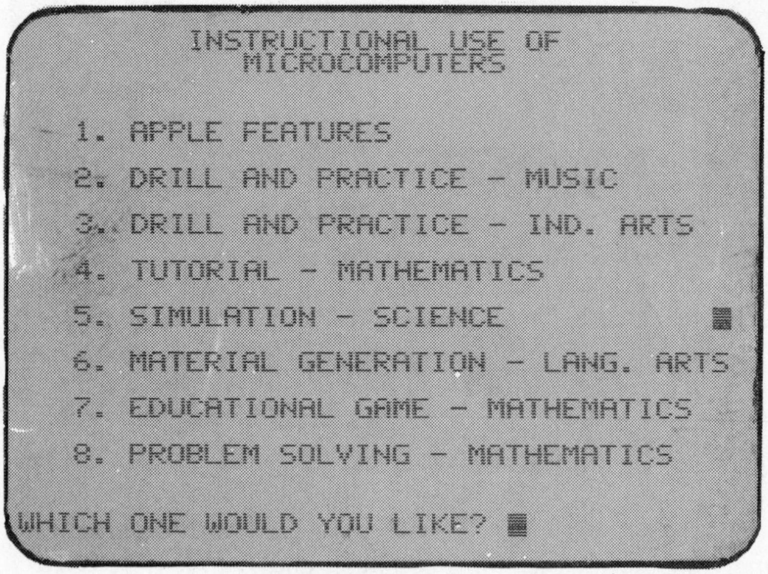

Figure 11-5

A floppy disk commonly contains more than one program or "data file." The "menu" or "catalog" of the disk serves as the Table of Contents. Some libraries may find it useful to have the contents listed:

```
371.33    MECC Apple demonstration [machine-readable data
MEC          file] / Minnesota Educational Computing
             Consortium -- St. Paul : MECC, 1980.
             1 floppy disk (1 vol. version 1.1) + guide
             Use with Apple II microcomputer

             Contents: Apple features, drill and practice--
             music, drill and practice--ind. arts, tutorial
             --mathematics, simulation--science, material
             generation--lang. arts, educational games--
             mathematics, problem solving--mathematics.

             1.  Teaching material  I.  MECC
       II.  Title:  Apple demonstration
```

Or a brief summary of the contents:

```
371.33    MECC  Apple demonstration [machine-readable data
MEC          file] / Minnesota Educational Computing
             Consortium -- St. Paul : MECC, 1980.
             1 floppy disk (1 vol. version 1.1) + guide
             Use with Apple II microcomputer

             Summary: a series of brief demonstrations
             illustrating the Apple II's instructional
             application in five curriculum areas--music,
             industrial arts, math, science, language
             arts

             1.  Teaching material  I.  MECC
       II.  Title:  Apple demonstration
```

SUMMARY

Original cataloging, adapting copy, and preparing reports requires professional training and attention. There are other tasks, however, such as stamping, typing, lettering, and pasting that must also be done if materials are to be shelved ready for circulation. Even systems with central processing require some of the procedures to be done at the local library, and although these are often the responsibility of volunteers, student assistants, and clerks, efficient organization and planning are necessary if they are to be fitted into the work schedule.

No matter how catalog copy is acquired, the individual library is responsible for analytics and *see* and *see also* references. It is probably best not to make analytics routinely but to rely on published indexes when possible. But those analytics

139

or cross references that give service to the patron and save time for the librarian should be provided.

If such materials as serials, kits, maps, and computer software are to be cataloged, they require special attention. Serial entries must reflect library holdings, maps need scale location, kits are often more useful if broken into components, and few directions have, as yet, been given for new formats such as floppy disks.

Since a misfiled card may mean an unused item, filing should only be done by those who understand the structure of the catalog. The 1980 ALA rules simplify filing for those libraries that adopt them and make more sense to patrons accustomed to using less complicated files.

CHAPTER REVIEW

Terms to remember:

analytic entries	numeric area
first indention	open entry
floppy disk	second indention
kit	third indention
mathematical data area	

Preparation:

Prepare material for circulation by typing pocket and card. Maintain card catalog by shifting cards, furnishing guide cards and labels.

Typing cards:

Prepare standard guidelines for indention and formats.

Analytics:

When practical provide access to parts of the content of material, either by author of a part, subject of a part, or title of a part.

Special materials:

Maintain accurate serial cataloging by recording serials owned.

Record scale of maps important enough to be cataloged.

When kits are more useful processed and cataloged by parts, do so.

Floppy disks can be described at level one, recording other necessary information in the notes.

CHAPTER 12

THE MICROCOMPUTER AND THE CATALOGER

THE PURPOSE of the catalog — to answer questions about the library collection, and the aim of the cataloger — to organize library materials for reader access — have not changed since the earliest days. To meet the growing need for information in contemporary society librarians are turning, as they have always done, to the latest technology.

COMPUTERS AND CATALOGING

Certain characteristics of computers make them ideal tools for certain library tasks. Computers are accurate, consistent, and speedy workhorses that can, by performing routine tasks, free people for other types of activity. When used in the cataloging process, for example, computers can reduce duplication of effort.

When bibliographic information is stored in a card, book, or COM catalog a separate record must be created for each access point. The more access the users are given, the more expensive the process becomes. When information is stored in the data base of a computer, however, it need be stored only once. That record can then be manipulated, sorted, and accessed in a number of ways to serve a variety of functions, from accounting procedures to cataloging. But, if single records are going to be used for many activities, all of the information required must be available in that record. Therefore, data is transcribed into an automated system according to more exacting standards than in a manual system.

For a number of years, the Library of Congress has been experimenting through the MARC program to find the best ways to record bibliographic data. Today there are exacting standards for conversion of cataloging records into machine readable form. Huge data bases of catalog information, based on the MARC format, have been created and are maintained by bibliographic services. Because computers can communicate with each other, it is possible for many libraries to obtain their cataloging from these large data bases through net-working. Fully automated cataloging is expensive, and in the past large libraries have been the principal users of these services.

The last few years have seen a flood of publicity for the MICROCOMPUTER, a small, inexpensive computer that can stand on a desk. Like MAIN FRAME computers, the microcomputer is an instrument that can store and manipulate information of any kind. But unlike large computers, microcomputers are available in every shopping mall. The mystery of seeing and touching a computer is gone, and today's computer literate is as likely to be a nine-year-old as a Nobel prize winner. Library patrons will soon be demanding access to the catalog through a computer keyboard. In many small and medium-sized collections the microcomputer can be used to provide such access.

Microcomputers cannot, at present, store the millions of bibliographic records a large library needs. However, just as not every library needs records at the second or third levels of description, few libraries need access to large data bases. In such circumstances the microcomputer offers a number of advantages.

1. Microcomputers are small and need no special environmental controls. They can be installed in the library and controlled by the library staff.

2. Their cost is relatively low, and constantly decreasing.

3. Because microcomputers are small and fairly simple to program, they can perform operations that were previously considered either too small, or too specialized, to automate.

4. Microcomputers can be integrated with large computers to form a complete information system for a library.

Customized subject access can now be provided through automation to users of specialized collections. This could be the most fruitful area for microcomputer application. By using general subject heading lists and standardized access points, catalogers hope to provide access to the general public, but specialized needs have been too expensive to consider. Access by reading level, for example, might be of much more use to a teacher than access by author or title. Church libraries need supplementary subject headings in areas such as the Bible. Psychologists could use materials more readily if they were cataloged by learning domains. The microcomputer allows subject headings to be created quickly and deleted as necessary.

143

CLERICAL SUPPORT   Few of the purposes of a library could be achieved without strong clerical support. Once only large libraries could use automation for housekeeping chores, but now the microcomputer can assist those with small collections.

1. Whatever the manner of cataloging, authority files for names, subjects, and cross references need to be maintained. By storing these on a computer disk, time spent in filing and updating is reduced.

2. The computer can generate information from its data base in a variety of forms, including printed cards, pockets, labels, and other processing necessities.

3. Inventory records can be maintained.

4. Bibliographies can be prepared on request from users.

5. Many circulation chores can be handled by the computer: charge records, overdue notices, reserve notices, statistical reports.

LIBRARIANS AND AUTOMATION

The tasks and services the computer can perform in a library are limited only by the software, or programs, given to the equipment. Because these instructions are normally written by a programmer, librarians may feel a loss of control with the introduction of this new technology. This feeling may be compounded when those in the know converse in "computerese." A library can profit from automation only if the librarians understand what tasks a computer can perform, which of these tasks the library needs the computer to do, and what hardware (equipment) is necessary for the job.

Computers can perform almost any kind of information-handling task, including storing, rearranging, indexing, sorting and alphabetizing, and printing out. Before they can do any of these, instructions, or programs must be entered into their memory. Normally these instructions are written by computer programmers, but they cannot successfully do this unless the librarian explains the task to them. When library computer applications fail, the cause is often either failure to communicate to the programmer exactly what is wanted, or lack of understanding of what was possible in the first place.

After the program is completed it must be INPUT into the computer's memory. With a microcomputer this is either through a keyboard, an audiocassette tape, or a floppy disk. Different hardware is required for each. The program is necessary to tell the computer what to do with the data that the library staff will input. This data may be names of borrowers, authority files, cataloging records, or any information necessary for the computer to do the task that it has been programmed for. The information may be input in a number of ways: by a light pen, another computer, by voice, or by typing. Inputting data, especially when it is done manually, can be time-consuming and therefore expensive. That is why it is imperative that each task, before it is turned over to a computer, be analyzed and evaluated as a candidate for automation.

After the computer has manipulated the data according to its instructions, it will produce an OUTPUT. This may be in the form of a microform or hard copy, a visual display on a screen, a machine output for another computer, or a configuration. Depending on how the library wishes to use the information, a visual display could serve for an on-line catalog, a printed list for a bibliography, or for overdue notices.

PLANNING THE SYSTEM

As the cost of the microcomputer continues to fall and its storage capacity to increase, even large libraries with access to main frame computers, will find it more convenient to take care of many chores with the microcomputer. Conversely, small independent libraries serving churches, schools, and hospitals may have a need to go outside their own small local data base and seek information from another system. Microcomputers can be programmed to interface with other computer systems, and church, school, or other libraries can network as they wish.

Almost any library wishing to automate one or more of its systems can now find a model library close by, articles and books pointing the way, and vendors eager to lend their services. The library must still take that first step, however, and libraries that have a history of poor planning are unlikely to be successful with computer application. Pitfalls to avoid include:

1. Poor systems planning. When little attention has been paid to the way a manual system operates, it is unlikely to be successful when automated. There should be an evident need for automation and an analysis of functions. Automation fails when the librarian assumes details of a procedure are obvious and need not be analyzed or explained.

2. Tendency to stay with the old ways. When personnel is hostile, fearful, or untrained in library automation, sophisticated technology matters little.

3. Unrealistic vendor promises. Many computer firms do not recognize the peculiarities of library operation and may promote an address list program. Librarians seeking to buy a solution to a problem, not just a program, should do their homework, and shop around.

4. Lack of understanding of concepts. Automation should be done with a view to what the computer can do, not in order to change manual systems. Librarians have often deferred to technical people, rather than explaining their needs in terms of automation. Librarians should learn the computer meaning of such terms as "file," "storage," and "record."

SUMMARY

Many large libraries have been using computers to retrieve cataloging information and record circulation and acquisition records for some time. The availability of the microcomputer now means smaller libraries or those with specialized needs can do the same. Microcomputers offer many advantages over the large main frames, including local control, lower cost, application to smaller, simpler systems, flexibility, and ability to interface with large systems.

Successful microcomputer application, like successful main frame application, relies on the librarian's ability to apply systems design, to communicate with the data-processing professional, to understand the logical aspects of automation, and to negotiate with vendors. The rewards are an ability to handle increased volume of activity, more control over operations and collections, ability to provide new services, to prevent duplication of effort, and finally, and most important, improved service to users.

TYPING SUGGESTIONS

When faced with the chore of typing a set of catalog cards it is little comfort to know these occasions have become less frequent during the past decade. Directions for spacing and punctuation have been given elsewhere in this book; this section summarizes typing procedures.

Spacing between lines
Lines should be separated by single spacing, but leave two lines between the physical description and the notes, and at least three lines between end of catalog information and tracings.

Accent marks
If the typewriter has accent marks, type as written; otherwise add in ink.

Capitalization
In general, follow common usage, i.e., capitalize proper names and words derived from proper names, titles of people, historic events, first word of a sentence, or the beginning of a title of a work. Do not capitalize parts of titles that are not proper nouns.
In a title main entry, if the title begins with an article, the following word is also capitalized.

Abbreviations
Abbreviate standard terms as listed in the appendix.
Abbreviate names of states following names of places.
Abbreviate names of countries following foreign places.

Call numbers
Type the classification number on the third line from the top of the card, two spaces from the left-hand edge.
Type Cutter number, or book number, directly below the classification number.
Type any additional parts, such as date or volume number, directly below book numbers.
Use no punctuation except for the decimal in the class number, or a period after "v." (volume).

147

Series

Begin series area (in parentheses) after a full stop following physical description area.

Use no capitalization except for first word of series and for proper names.

If the series area runs over the line, return to first indention on next line.

Notes

When used, notes begin two lines below the physical description, starting at the second indention.

Given in paragraph form, each note beginning a new line at second indention and continuing at first indention if it runs over.

In content notes, standard ISBD punctuation is followed.

Tracings

Arrange in paragraph form.

Type these at least three lines below the catalog information at first indention.

If there is no room on the face of the card, type them on the back of the card near the bottom, so the card can be tilted forward and the tracings easily read.

Tracings are numbered: arabic numbers for subjects, roman numerals for added entries.

Tracings should be typed on the main entry card and on the shelf list card.

Added cards

If there is too much information to go on one catalog card, it is continued on a second card. Type at the point of break: "Continued on next card."

On the second card type the call number, the main entry, title and date. In parentheses, add "Card 2" two spaces below contents.

Use of stamps

Never type when a stamp will do. Frequently used information, such as "Ask at desk," or "Reference," can be stamped either above the call number or as a note.

COMPLETING
PREPARED
PRINTED CARDS

1. The Main Entry Card.
   Leave one card as is except for typing in the call number. This is the main entry card.
2. Subject Cards.
   When making a subject card, type the subject heading one line above the main entry at second indention.

Type subject headings in capital letters, spelling all words in full, including those abbreviated in the tracing.

If the subject will occupy more than one line, begin at the second line above the main entry, and begin the run-on line directly below at the second indention.

3. Name-Added Entries.

If, after a name, there is a designation "joint author," it follows after the name of the person in the added entry card.

4. Title Entries.

The word "title" in the tracings indicates that a title card is an added entry. On the line above the main entry, beginning at second indention, type the title. If it runs onto the second line, start two lines above the main entry and continue on the next line at the third indention.

5. Series.

If there is an entry made for a series, only the word "series" is found in the tracings. In that case, type the series title above the main entry matching the series title as given in the series area on the card.

TYPING A COMPLETE SET OF CARDS

When all the cards must be typed, prepare only the shelf list and main entry card in full. On all other added entry cards, stop after recording the date. This produces a truncated record. Users can see the whole record on the main entry card.

General abbreviations that are standard usage in cataloging:

abridged	abr.
approximately	approx.
black and white	b & w
book	bk.
centimeters	cm.
chapter	ch.
colored, coloured	col.
company	co.
compiler	comp.
copyright	c.
corporation	corp.
edition	ed.
enlarged	enl.
frame	fr.
illustration(s)	ill.
introduction	introd.
Limited	Ltd.
no name of place	s.l.
no name of publisher	s.n.
photographs	photos
preface	pref.
revised	rev.
series	ser.
silent	si.
sound	sd.
supplement	suppl.
volume(s)	v.

ALA Filing Rules. Filing Committee Resources and Technical Services Division. American Library Association. Chicago, American Library Association, 1980.

Anglo-American Cataloging Rules. 2nd ed. Edited by Michael Gorman and Paul Winkler. Chicago, American Library Association, 1978.

Arksley, Laura. "The Library of Assurbanipal." *Wilson Library Bulletin 51* (June 1977), pp. 833-840.

Austin, Derek and Jeremy A. Digger. "PRECIS: The Preserved Context Index System." *Library Resources and Technical Services,* 21: 13-30 (Winter 1977).

Barden, Bertha R. *Book Numbers: A Manual for Students with a Basic Code of Rules.* Chicago, American Library Association, 1932.

Bloomberg, Marty and Hans Weber. *An Introduction to Classification and Number Building in Dewey.* Libraries Unlimited, 1976.

Bloomberg, Marty. *Introduction to Technical Services for Library Technicians.* By Marty Bloomberg and G. Edward Evans. Third ed. Littleton, Colo., Libraries Unlimited, Inc., 1976.

Chan, Lois Mai. *Cataloging and Classification: An Introduction.* New York, McGraw-Hill, 1981.

Clark, Doris Hargrett. *The Making of a Code: The Issues Underlying AACR2.* Chicago, American Library Association, 1980.

Curley, Arthur and Jean Varlejs. *Aker's Simple Library Cataloging.* 6th ed. Scarecrow, 1977.

Cutter, Charles A. *Alphabetic Order Table Altered and Fitted with Three Figures by Kate Sanborn.* (Obtained from H. R. Huntting Co., Chicopee Falls, Mass.)

Dewey, Melvil. *Dewey Decimal Classification and Relative Index.* 19th ed. Lake Placid Club, N.Y., Forest Press, Inc. of Lake Placid Club Education Foundation, 1979. 3 v.

Dewey, Melvil. *Dewey Decimal Classification and Relative Index.* 11th abridged ed. Lake Placid Club, N.Y., Forest Press, Inc. of Lake Placid Club Education Foundation, 1979.

Dowell, Arlene Taylor. *Cataloging with Copy, A Decision-Maker's Handbook.* Littleton, Colo., Libraries Unlimited, Inc., 1976.

Dunkin, Paul S. *Cataloging U.S.A.* Chicago, American Library Association, 1969.

Library of Congress. *Classification Class A-Z.* Washington, Government Printing Office, 1904 to date.

Library of Congress. *Subject Headings Used in the Dictionary Catalogs of the Library of Congress.* Washington, Subject Cataloging Division, Processing Department, Library of Congress.

Malinconico, S. Michael. *The Future of the Catalog: the Library's Choices.* By S. Michael Malinconico and Paul J. Fasara. White Plains, New York, Knowledge Industry Publications, Inc., 1979.

Maltby, Arthur. *Classification in the 1970s: A Second Look.* Edited by Arthur Maltby. Rev. ed. London, C. Bingley, 1976.

Maltby, Arthur. *Sayers' Manual of Classification for Librarians.* 5th ed. London, Grafton, 1975.

Marshall, Joan. *On Equal Terms: a Thesaurus for Non-Sexist Indexing and Cataloging.* New York, Neal-Schuman, 1977.

Matthews, Joseph D. *Choosing an Automated Library System: A Planning Guide.* Chicago, American Library Association, 1980.

Maxwell, Margaret. *Handbook for AACR2: Explaining and Illustrating Anglo-American Cataloging Rules.* 2nd ed. American Library Association, 1980.

Miller, Edward. *Prince of Librarians: the Life and Times of Antonio Panizzi of the British Museum.* Athens, Ohio, Ohio University Press, 1974.

Norris, Dorothy May. *A History of Cataloguing and Cataloguing Methods 1100-1880: With an Introductory Survey of Ancient Times.* London, Grafton, 1936.

Olson, Nancy B. *Cataloging of Audiovisual Materials; a Manual Based on AACR2.* Mankato, Minn., Minnesota Scholarly Press, 1981.

Painter, Ann F. *Comparative Reader in Classification and Descriptive Cataloging.* Washington, NCR Microcard Edition, 1972.

Piercy, Esther J. *Commonsense Cataloging.* 2nd ed. Rev. by Marion Sanner. New York, H. W. Wilson, 1974.

Schmidt, Charles J. *Tapping Multi-Use Mainframe Systems.* Macon, Georgia, Middle Georgia Regional Library, 1980.

Sears List of Subject Headings. 12th ed. Edited by Barbara M. Westby. New York, H. W. Wilson, 1982.

Subject Retrieval in the Seventies: New Directions: Proceedings of an International Symposium. Hans (Hana) Wellisch, Thomas D. Wilson, eds. Westport, Conn., Greenwood Publishing Co., Published in conjunction with the School of Library and Information Services, University of Maryland, 1972.

Young, Micki Jo. *Introduction to Microcomputers in Federal Libraries.* By Micki Jo Young. With Frank A. Pezzanite and J. Chris Reisinger. Washington, Library of Congress, 1978.

American Book Publishing Record (BPR). New York, R. R. Bowker Company, 1960 to date.

Book Review Digest. New York, H. W. Wilson Company, 1905 to date.

The Booklist. Chicago, American Library Association, 1905 to date.

Children's Catalog. 14th ed. New York, H. W. Wilson Company, 1981.

Fiction Catalog. 10th ed. New York, H. W. Wilson Company, 1980.

Junior High School Library Catalog. 4th ed. New York, H. W. Wilson Company, 1980.

Public Library Catalog. 7th ed. New York, H. W. Wilson Company, 1978.

Senior High School Library Catalog. 12th ed. New York, H. W. Wilson Company, 1982, 1214 p.

Weekly Record. New York, R. R. Bowker Company, 1974 to date. Weekly.

ACCESS POINT—A term under which a bibliographic record is filed.

ACCESSION NUMBER—A number assigned to each item in order of its receipt in the library.

ADDED ENTRY—A catalog entry other than the main or subject entry; includes titles, joint authors, series, etc.

ALTERNATIVE TITLE—A second title introduced by "or" or its equivalent.

ANALYTIC ENTRY—A catalog entry for a part of a work, entered under the author, title, or subject of the part.

ANGLO-AMERICAN CATALOGING RULES, 2nd ed. (AACR2)— The official American cataloging code, covering both description and access points for eleven formats of materials.

AREA TABLE—Table II notations from the DDC applied to other notations to designate geographical areas.

AUTHOR ENTRY—The name of the author of a work used as the filing name in the catalog; often the main entry.

AUTHORITY FILE—A record of names or terms used as catalog entries; maintained in order to insure uniformity.

AUTHOR SERIES—A series of books written by one author and issued under a collective title.

BASE NUMBER—From the DDC. That portion of a number in a sequence which does not vary as other digits are added as instructed.

BIBLIOGRAPHIC DETAILS—Those features of a work such as title, author, edition, publisher, date, and series used for identification and description.

BIBLIOGRAPHIC UTILITY—A service organization that maintains large on-line files of bibliographic data.

BOOK CATALOG—A library catalog in the form of a book.

BOOK NUMBER—Part of a call number used to arrange materials with the same classification number in alphabetical order.

CALL NUMBER—The number (composed of letters, numbers, and symbols) used to identify and locate a library item.

CARD CATALOG—A library catalog of cards. An entry, or record, is placed on each card.

CATALOGING IN PUBLICATION (CIP)—Cataloging data on the verso of the title page, furnished by the Library of Congress.

CATALOGING PROFILE — Cataloging and/or processing specifications developed for an individual library.

CLAIMING — The process of notifying a jobber, subscription service, or publisher that serial issues are missing.

CLASSED CATALOG — A catalog arranged by subject or classification number.

CLASSIFICATION — The grouping of materials by subject or form, usually according to the DDC or the LCC.

CLOSED SHELVES — Areas housing library materials that are not accessible to the public.

COLLECTION — A distinct group of books or other materials; may refer to a library's entire holdings.

COLLECTIVE WORK — An item that contains either three or more independent parts by one author or two or more independent parts by more than one author.

COLLECTIVE TITLE — An inclusive title under which several works, each of which may have an individual title, are published.

COM CAT — Computer output microform catalog. A catalog produced by a computer either on fiche or microfilm.

CORPORATE ENTRY — The name of a corporate body used as a catalog entry.

CROSS REFERENCES — Referrals from terms or names not used in a particular catalog or index to those that are. See *See* and *See also*.

CUTTER TABLE — A list of letters and numbers assigned to names of authors to form parts of call numbers.

DDC — The Dewey Decimal Classification system; a system of notation used to classify library materials.

DESCRIPTIVE CATALOGING — Providing a description and establishing access points for library materials.

DICTIONARY CATALOG — A catalog in which all entries, including authors, titles, and subjects, are filed in a single alphabet.

DIVIDED CATALOG — A catalog divided into parts. Usually one part contains author, title, and other added entries, and a second part has subject entries.

DUPLICATE — An item identical to another in content, format, etc. Often used to refer to additional copies of a work.

EASY BOOK — A book for young children, usually consisting primarily of pictures.

EDITION — The entire number of identical copies of a work published at the same time

ENTRY — A bibliographic record of an item in a catalog.

FILING TITLE — A standard title assigned to a work that has appeared under various titles to identify it in the catalog.

FIRST INDENTION—The distance from the left-hand edge of the catalog card at which the main entry begins.

FIXED LOCATION—An arrangement of library materials in which each item is assigned a permanent location.

FLOPPY DISK—A small record-like, paper-encased plastic disk that stores information.

GENERAL MATERIALS DESIGNATIONS [GMD]—A term indicating a broad, general class of material to which an item belongs, e.g., text, microform, etc.

HANGING INDENTION—The form used for a catalog card on which the title is the main entry and is the only line on the card beginning at the first indention.

HEADING—Any word, name, or phrase placed at the head of a catalog entry to provide an access point.

INPUT—Getting a program into the computer's memory, normally through a keyboard, a cassette tape recorder, or a disk drive.

INTER-LIBRARY LOAN—Exchange of materials between libraries.

INTERNATIONAL STANDARD BIBLIOGRAPHIC DESCRIPTION (ISBD)—An international standard of punctuation for bibliographic records.

INTERNATIONAL STANDARD BOOK NUMBER (ISBN)—A code number uniquely assigned to a specific title or edition of a title.

INTERNATIONAL STANDARD SERIAL NUMBER (ISSN)—A code number uniquely assigned to a series.

KIT—A multi-media item.

LCC—Library of Congress Cataloging.

LCSH—*Library of Congress Subject Headings.* Used in many college and university libraries.

MAIN ENTRY—A complete catalog record of an item under the heading by which it will be uniformly identified.

MAIN FRAME—A large, powerful computer, capable of controlling other computer systems.

MARC—A data base of cataloging information distributed by the Library of Congress.

MATHEMATICAL DATA AREA—An area of descriptive cataloging, used only for cartographic material, in which scale and projection are recorded.

MICROCOMPUTER—The smallest computer system, designed for a single user.

MICROFICHE—A microform issued as a card.

MICROFILM—A microform issued in a continuous strip.

MICROFORM CATALOG—A catalog produced in microform

(either microfilm or microfiche) in a size too small to be read by the naked eye.

MIXED RESPONSIBILITY — A work to which several people (e.g., author and illustrator) contributed.

MNEMONIC — A device intended to assist the memory.

NET-WORKING — Organizing libraries in order to share bibliographic data and materials.

NUMERIC AND/OR ALPHABETIC DESIGNATION — An area of descriptive cataloging that applies only to serials.

OCLC — A bibliographic network that shares cataloging between member libraries via on-line terminals.

OMNI CATALOG — A catalog in which records of all formats are found.

ON-LINE COMPUTER CATALOG — Distribution of cataloging information by on-line computer transmission.

OPEN ENTRY — A catalog entry for a serial or set which has not yet completed publication; certain information will be filled in later.

OPEN SHELF — Library materials in areas open to the public.

ORIGINAL CATALOGING — The process of creating a catalog record without prepared copy supplied by a vendor.

OTHER TITLE INFORMATION — Any title on an item that is neither the title proper nor a parallel title.

OUTPUT — Supplying the results of the computer's work to the user.

PARALLEL TITLE — The title proper in another language or script.

PERIODICAL — A publication with a distinctive title intended to appear in successive numbers or parts at stated or regular intervals and for an indefinite time.

PHOENIX SCHEDULE — A completely new schedule in the DDC. Only the basic number for the discipline remains the same.

PHYSICAL DESCRIPTION — Identifying the physical characteristics of an item for cataloging purposes.

PRECIS — The Preserved Context Indexing System, a chain indexing system used to provide subject access to *The British National Bibliography.*

PUBLISHER SERIES — A series of books by different authors issued under a collective title.

RELATIVE INDEX — An index that reverses the subordination of subject to discipline by bringing together aspects of subjects from the disciplines used in classification.

RELATIVE LOCATION — A system of arranging library materials that allows new material to be intershelved at any point.

SCHEDULES — The notations of the ten main classes of the Dewey Decimal Classification system.

SCOPE NOTE — A note in DDC, *Sears*, or LCC explaining the limitations or special qualifications of a subject or notation.

SEARS — The *Sears List of Subject Headings*; used in many schools.

SECOND INDENTION — The distance from the left-hand edge of the catalog card at which the title begins.

SEE ALSO REFERENCE — An instruction guiding the reader from a name or term to others which are related to it.

SEE REFERENCE — An instruction guiding the reader from a name or term not used to one which is to be found in the catalog or reference work.

SERIAL — A publication issued in successive parts and intended to be continued indefinitely; includes such items as periodicals, newspapers, reports, and bulletins.

SHELF LIST — A file that is arranged in the same order as the items on the shelf.

SPECIFIC MATERIALS DESCRIPTION — A term that indicates the specific or special class of material to which an item belongs, e.g., filmstrips, microfiche, etc.

SPECIFIC SUBJECT ENTRY — Assigning a heading that deals with the specific subject of an item, not the general class.

STANDARD SUBDIVISIONS — Table I from the DDC: notations indicating recurring forms that may be added to notations from the schedules.

SUBJECT HEADING — An access point, or heading, appearing at the top of an entry, that identifies the topic of a work.

SUPPLIED TITLE — A title supplied by a cataloger to identify those items that have no title.

TABLES — A sequence of notations used in classification systems.

TECHNICAL READING — An examination of certain parts of an item, especially the Chief Source of Information, as part of the cataloging process.

THESAURUS — An index of terms used in information retrieval, especially from a computer.

THIRD INDENTION — The distance from the left-hand edge of a catalog card at which the description begins.

TITLE ENTRY — The catalog entry under the title of a publication.

TITLE PROPER — The chief name of an item, including an alternative title, but not other title information.

TRACINGS — Items listed on the main entry catalog record indicating other entries that have been made and filed for the same work.

TRUNCATED RECORD — A record that has been shortened.

UNIFORM HEADING — A particular heading by which a work is to be identified for cataloging purposes.

UNIFORM TITLE — A particular title for a work with several variant titles. Also a conventional collective title used for volumes containing several works.

UNION CATALOG — A catalog indexing the holdings of groups of libraries or information centers.

UNIT SET — A set of catalog entries identical except for the headings or access points.

VENDOR — A jobber or wholesaler of materials used in libraries.

VERSO — The left-hand page in an open book.

VISIBLE FILE — A series of metal frames in which cards may be mounted with the headings showing one above another; used by libraries as a checking file for material received, and as a catalog record for periodicals.

WORD-BY-WORD FILING — Filing that observes the spaces at the end of each word.